D1826727

THE PORTRAIT

Also by Ethel M. Gray:
The Diplomatic Mission of Rivadavia in Great Britain
The English Reader
El Estudio Literario de la Biblia

THE PORTRAIT

Ethel M. Gray

The Book Guild Ltd
Sussex, England

This book is sold subject to the condition that it shall not, by way of trade or otherwise, be lent, re-sold, hired out, photocopied or held in any retrieval system, or otherwise circulated without the publisher's prior consent in any form of binding or cover other than that in which this is published and without a similar condition including this condition being imposed on the subsequent purchaser.

The Book Guild Limited
Temple House
25 High Street
Lewes, Sussex

First published 1991
© Ethel M. Gray 1991
Set in Baskerville
Typesetting by Hawks Phototypesetters
Copthorne, West Sussex
Printed in Great Britain by
Antony Rowe Ltd
Chippenham

British Library Cataloguing in Publication Data
Gray, Ethel M. (Ethel Mary) 1912-
    The portrait.
    1. Jesus Christ
    I. Title
    232

ISBN 0 86332 565 3

"A glory gilds the sacred page
    Majestic, like the sun:
It gives a light to every age,
    It gives, but borrows none.

The hand that gave it still supplies
    The gracious light and heat:
Its truths upon the nations rise;
    They rise, but never set.

Let everlasting thanks be Thine
    For such a bright display
As makes the world of darkness shine
    With beams of heavenly day.

My soul rejoices to pursue
    The steps of Him I love.
Till glory breaks upon my view
    In brighter worlds above!"

                            W. Cowper

"Looking upon Jesus as He walked"

... *John 1:36.*

CONTENTS

MEDITATIONS ON THE MEDITATOR

PREFACE

There grew upon the present writer through years of the loving study of the Psalms the conviction that in them lay hidden a portrait of Him we know as Jesus in the Gospels, and indeed in the New Testament as a whole. These notes are the search for and became the gradual disclosure of that secret Portrait.

On the ground that by examining not merely a single work but an author's whole output one may build up a portrait of the man himself, and that the study of a poem should seek the meaning it held for its author, it seemed but logical to apply the same practice to a study of the Psalms.

But there was the primary obstacle of their multiple authorship. The decision was therefore made to examine first only those of David, though the main motive was not to obtain a portrait of David's character but the desire to find out if the thoughts attributable to Christ might be found, not only in the known 'Messianic' psalms but in the Psalms as a whole, or at least in the conjuction of David's. The fascinating question posed was: would a mental portrait of Christ emerge from a study of *all* the Psalms as messianic. These notes do not seek to dogmatize but to explore, and were composed as progress was made along what was so far as I knew an untrodden path, for even after careful research no material could be found to prove that this road had been travelled before.

Though the attempt was at first limited to the search for a portrait of the Messiah in the psalms of His earthly ancestor, there remained the fact that, faith having accepted all Scripture as inspired by the Holy Spirit, a single

9

Authorship is thereby acknowledged, and hence a single Mind formulated the whole. On that basis it should be possible to trace some part of that Portrait in *every* Psalm. Thus the guiding principle of the examination was simply belief in the divine inspiration of the Psalms, this to include even their placing and sequence.

One had always thought of David as the Warrior King, God-chosen founder of the lineage of which His Son should be born, and the 'Sweet singer of Israel', but not as a prophet. But Matthew spoke of 'the prophet David', referring to Psalm 22:18. So the attempt to seek a prophetic significance in all David's psalms, if and where it existed, seemed justifiable, my premise being that this could not be limited to those psalms generally accepted as 'Messianic', such as the 22nd. It seemed possible that when the author of the Epistle to the Hebrews speaks of the Holy Ghost *'saying in David'* (Heb. 3:7;4:7) he might not mean merely 'in the psalms of David' (as one would say 'in Dickens') but that he could be interpreted as meaning 'in the person of David'.

Further, it may be said that David suffered messianically (how else express it?) when he wrote such psalms as the 16th, 22nd, 69th, whether it were from actual experience, or vision. When such a burden of prophecy overshadowed him he must have asked when 'entering into the cloud' as it were, the question in Psalms 42 and 43: 'Why art thou cast down, O my soul?' — unaware that the prophetic spirit upon him was causing him to voice (or write) words that would later more aptly express the unspoken feelings of the Messiah. Of course David could have been 'cast down' by his own struggles and disappointments in his sons and friends, but the forcefully repeated question addressed to his soul seems to formulate a challenge of profounder import.

The references to the Psalms in the Epistle to the Hebrews are *about* the Messiah. The aim of my search was to discover *what thoughts* might have been in His mind, especially at certain moments of His earthly experience such as those described in Psalm 22. There must surely be other psalms that go behind the scenes as this one does. Together, they might give an inside picture of the life of Christ and disclose a portrait of His inner life.

A reverent forbearance restrained my quest, however, and the fear of presumption, lest what I sought was not for men to know, since it has not been revealed in the writings of the Evangelists. The veil screening the Holiest was rent, giving free access to the Ark of the Covenant, but was it permissible to look within? Perhaps not. Yet if the study were approached with deference and prayer for the guidance of the Holy Spirit, surely that which was to be withheld would still be so. Paul declares his highest aim to be to 'know HIM', and the Almighty Himself frequently invites men to come to Him whom to know is life eternal and the purest delight that man can attain. 'But let him that glorieth glory in this, that he understandeth and knoweth me'. (Jer. 9:24). God tells what is in His mind: 'I will raise me up a faithful priest, that shall do according to that which is in my heart, and in my mind.' (I Sam.2:35). 'You give your sons for burnt offerings . . . which I commanded not . . . neither came it into my mind'. (Jer. 19:5). 'For my thoughts are not as your thoughts . . , saith the Lord'. (Isa. 55:8). 'For I know the thoughts that I think toward you, saith the Lord, thoughts of peace and not of evil, to give you an expected end.' (Jer. 29:11). His thoughts are 'very deep' (Psa. 92:5) and 'cannot be reckoned' (Psa. 40:5); we cannot expect to plumb them, but we may try to know some of them. Incredible as it seems, according to I Cor. 2:16 it is given to us who are His to have the very mind of Christ! Hence it cannot be unlawful to try to think His thoughts after Him.

In the Gospels we have an account of the life of Jesus viewed externally. Have we in the Psalms an account of the thoughts that He never spoke aloud? The study of them would reveal His inner life, the workings of His mind. To return to the analogy of the Ark of the Covenant; The contents of the Ark symbolized Christ and may be thought of as symbolizing His nature, for Jesus was the Manna sent down from Heaven; He was the Bread of Life. (Jn. 6:31-60), and His body did not see corruption (Psa. 16:10). He was the word that tastes as sweet as honey (Psa. 19), as did the Manna. With regard to the Tables of the Law: in the law was His delight (Psa. 1), He fulfilled all the law; it was perfect and unbroken in Him, for He 'fulfilled all righteousness' (Mat. 3:15). He meditated in the Law day and night (Psa. 19, 119, Mat. 4:4). and it was written in His heart, for He was God's Epistle. He was co-author with the Father of the Law and summed it up in the verb Love (Mat. 22:37; Mk. 12:28-34). The tables of the Law are also called the tables of the Covenant (Heb. 9:4): Christ was God's Covenant to men fulfilled. The third object, Aaron's rod that budded points to His eternal living, His physical life in perfection (cf. the Tree of life, Psa. 1; Jer. 17:7,8; Rev. 22:2). It indicates the full cycle of life — buds, blossoms and fruit, without the incidence of decay. Hebrews 9:4 gives this order: Aaron's rod, the tables of the covenant. Cf Exod. 16:33;25:21;40:20. Num.17:10 changed this. 'He put the testimony in the Ark', and Aaron's rod 'before the testimony'. In the end 'There was nothing in the Ark save the two tables of stone'. (I Ki. 8:9). All this was revealed.

The following Scriptures seem not only to justify the proposed search but to authorize it:-

We know that the Son of God has come, and hath *given us understanding that we may know Him* that is true. I John 5:20.

But *grow* in grace and *in the knowledge* of our Lord and Saviour Jesus Christ. II Pet. 3:18.

I count all things but loss for the *excellency of the knowledge of Christ Jesus my Lord . . . That I may know Him . . .* I follow after, if that I may apprehend that for which I am apprehended of Jesus Christ . . . *God shall reveal this unto you.* Phil. 3:8-15.

The Lord God . . . revealeth His secret unto His servants the prohets. Amos 3:7.

They shall be all taught of God. Isa. 54:13; John 6:45.

That the words might be fulfilled, which were spoken by *the prophet David*: They parted my garments among them. Mat. 27:35; Psa. 22:18.

The *prophet David.* Mat. 13:25; Psa. 78:2 — 'words spoken by the prophet saying, I will utter things *which have been kept secret* from the foundation of the world. . . . David being a prophet . . . Acts 2:30,31.

The Spirit of the Lord spake by me (David) and his word was in my tongue. II Sam. 23:2; Psa. 101.

He (Jesus) said unto them . . . All things must be

fulfilled, which were written in the law of Moses, and in the prophets, and *in the Psalms*, concerning me. Luke 24:44.

Take, my brethren, the prophets, who have spoken in the name of the Lord for an example of suffering affliction and of patience. James 5:10.

Again, he limited a certain day, *saying in David*, Today, if ye will hear my voice . . . Heb. 4:7; Psa. 95:7.

David himself said by the Holy Ghost, The Lord said unto my Lord . . . Psa. 110:1; Mat. 22:44, etc.

Men and brethren, let me freely speak unto you of the patriarch *David . . . being a prophet . . . spake of the resurrection of Christ* . . . Acts 2:29:-32.

Thou art God . . . who *by the mouth of thy servant David* hast said, Why do the heathen rage . . . etc. The rulers were gathered together against the Lord *and against His Christ* . . . Acts 4:24-36.

This scripture must needs have been fulfilled , *which the Holy Ghost by the mouth of David, spake* concerning Judas . . . Acts 1:16.

For it is written in the book of Psalms, Let his habitation be desolate (Psa. 69:25 — Let *their* habitation . . .) and his bishopric let another take. Psa. 109:8. Let another take his office (speaking of the 'wicked man') cf. Psa. 35:11, false witnesses. Acts 1:20.

How precious are *Thy thoughts* to me O God! How great is the sum of them! Psa. 139:17,18.

We speak the wisdom of God in a mystery, even the hidden wisdom . . . But *God hath revealed them unto us by His Spirit;* for the spirit searcheth all things, yea, *the deep things of God.* I Cor. 2:7-10.

I will shew thee that which is noted in the scripture of truth. Dan. 10:21.

In that hour Jesus rejoiced in spirit, and said, I thank Thee, O Father, Lord of heaven and earth, that Thou hast hid these things . . . and hast *revealed them unto babes:* even so Father, for so it seemed good in Thy sight. Luke 10:21.

. . . Who in the days of His flesh, when He had offered up prayers and *supplications with strong crying and tears* unto Him that was able to save Him from death, and was *heard in that He feared:* Though He were a Son, yet *learned He obedience by the things which He suffered:* and being made perfect, He became the author of eternal salvation. Heb. 5:7,8. (Note: In the Gospel account this is ratified only in Gethsemane. The full truth of these words must be sought in the Psalms).

☆   ☆   ☆

By one of those strange co-incidences which only come about by the guidance of the Holy Spirit, I was led to re-read the Gospel of Mark at the time of starting this study, and found that the sequence of events, so simply put forth in that Gospel, remarkably paralleled the thought and experiences of the first dozen or so of the Psalms. This gave the starting point for a purely empyric journey of exploration by coupling the incident with the Psalm, although this implied a hidden chronological order in their sequence and a developing experience as the link between them. Soon the other Gospels were found to offer the suggestive incident and background, and in the end every book in the Bible yielded its contribution, thus proving that the Psalms are not merely a collection of devout poems but an integral part of Holy Writ, closely interwoven with it.

The study then expanded by relating the experience in the Psalms to one or other of those of Jesus as reported in the Gospels or prophesied in the Old Testament and Revelation. Though imagination has helped at times, this has been kept under the strict discipline of the facts as given in the Scriptures.

A temporary halt became necessary at Psalm 51 and it seemed advisable to seek instruction from learned men of God whose knowledge of Hebrew and devout study of the Holy Word would point the way further. But on my perusal of as many of these works as were available, the majority were found to be expository on the verse-by-verse basis and were of no help at all in this particular search. It appeared that some of the early Church Fathers had remarked on the prophetic quality of the Psalms with regard to Messiah and His Church, but I was unable to consult them. For some structural hints Graham Scroggie's study of the Psalms was useful (often based on Thos. Boys' *A Key to the Psalms*) and the beautiful meditations of 'Christianus' (*The Christ of the*

Psalms), and Bellett: *Meditations on the Psalms*, were inspiring but were not directed toward the goal before me. Hence, though much spiritual enjoyment was derived from the writings of these and other authors (see Note), the only real guidance to be acknowledged is that of the Holy Scriptures themselves. Where help was received it has been acknowledged in the text. While revelling in this feast of reading, the realization became dominant that the present exploration must be continued independently, guided only by the Light which illumined the page and formed an ever-growing conviction that the mind of Christ would be found portrayed therein. The total absence of Oriental learning in these notes is to be regretted but its merit is that by its limitations this study is well within the scope of anyone willing to accept Holy Writ in its literal meaning. This requires faith as that of a little child.

For some passages use has been made of the J.B. Philips, Moffat, and Weymouth translations of the New Testament, and of the Old Testament in the New English version. These are named when cited.

As progress in the study unfolded the marvels of this veritable gallery of facets portraying One Central Figure, recognizably that of the Jesus of the Gospels, pause had frequently to be made in awe and adoration, to exclaim with Isaiah: 'I am undone . . . for mine eyes have seen the King!'

Some discoveries made during the study were at first startling. Take, for instance, the 88th, 130th, and 143rd Psalms, which are so obviously the cries of the Righteous Man's soul from Sheol. A clause in the Apostles' Creed affirms: ' . . . He descended into Hell . . .' The Apostles and the Fathers of the early Church believed this. Where had they learned it? 'Thou hast ascended into heaven', says Psa. 68:18, but not 'Thou hast descended into hell'. It is Paul who interprets this in a parenthesis: Now that he ascended, what is it but that he also descended first into the lower parts of the earth. (Eph. 4:9), but the Lord's own words did not go so far: No man hath ascended up to heaven but he that came down from heaven, even the Son of Man ... — speaking of His Incarnation, not His death. (John 3:13). The cry from 'the lowest parts of the earth', and 'from the pit' or Sheol, the 'dwelling in darkness', and so on, are found in the autobiographical psalms and nowhere else. These must be prophetic of the Messiah's experience though ostensibly they tell the author's, but he is of course alive at the time of the psalm's composition and could not really have entered the state of which the psalm tells with the vivid detail of an actual witness. Peter states that Jesus preached to the spirits in prison. Where did he get that information? If not directly from the lips of the risen Lord, it must have been from the Psalms. It was a widely held tenet of the Christian faith up till the end of the Middle Ages and found expression into the early Renaissance. Painters and sculptors depicted the 'Harrowing of Hell', purporting to show Christ defeating the powers of evil and releasing the souls of the just. This theme is found in art not only on the Continent but in early Saxon sculpture, in frescoes on English church walls, and in stained glass windows.

A book could be written on the subject of Christ's sojourn in Sheol as found in the Psalms, so much of it is there, and so vivid.

One marvels how such psalms ever got written down. During a dreadful spiritual experience like the sense of utter darkness, separation from God and confinement in a place far removed from 'the land of the living' — perhaps when David was a fugitive from Saul and living in a cave — we can imagine the words flowing into his mind, but he certainly would not have quill and parchment with him, hunted as he was from place to place, and fighting. And he did not carve them with a chisel on the walls of the cave or on slabs of stone to be carried about with him! Yet how were these psalms preserved so burningly *present* (they are all in the present tense) until they could be fixed in writing? The very existence of such a psalm, white-hot from the crucible, seems nothing less than miraculous, the Spirit's intention being to disclose prophetically the secret of what took place after the last witnessed scene, when 'It is finished' was spoken on earth.

Another wonder of the Psalms, as of all devotional parts of Scripture, is that the experiences undergone are so actual and ring so true by the witness of God's dealings with ourselves. The astonishing discovery had been that by projecting the Psalms into the mind of Christ (implemented by the Gospel narrative), it becomes evident that Jesus experienced the very same dealings. Thus our relationship with God is found to be very similar to that of the Son in His humanity (sin apart), and vice versa. Hence a richer meaning is read into John's words 'As many as received Him, to them gave He power to become (the) sons of God'. (1:2), 'NOW are we the sons of God'. We raise our hearts to the same Father. Jesus the Son of God might be thought of as above such suffering as for instance the sense of injustice and the hurt of people's tongues. But that He felt this as deeply as is humanly possible is evident in many of the Psalms, and thus He is drawn immeasurably closer.

A further spiritual truth believed but never apprehended clearly before and which becomes factual through these human-divine documents is that of God's unchanging Nature. He is for ever the Same. The various psalmists' experiences of God when attributed to Jesus, our own hearts ratifying the witness, brings this truth out. The path traced by our own spiritual experience paralleling that of the psalmist in his approach to God indisputably proves God's reality and His immutability, because it is not merely that our emotions in certain circumstances are similar to the psalmist's (and that Christ shared similar ones). Rather it is that the Holy Spirit has wrought in us in such a way as to bring us to the same experience of God. The space of time intervening between the composition of the psalm and its verifying in Christ, or between either and the present moment, disappears. This produces a powerful realization of God's timelessness. The Holy Spirit will continue to operate in men in the world in times as far removed from us perhaps as ours from the psalmist. One may imagine the believing Remnant in the last days brought by the relevance of these psalms to the same state of worship and rapture as was experienced by David so many centuries before, and that when we gather in God's Presence it will be to find that all have been conformed to the same Image

— His own.

And every virtue we possess
And every conquest won,
And every thought of holiness
Are His alone.

☆　　　☆　　　☆

During the study it was found that a sequence of thought bound certain psalms together into groups. This may be attributed to occasions such as national events or a season of spiritual disturbance during which the writer expressed himself in certain imagery although with developing thought. Such are the psalms of Asaph, (73-83). Yet the same evidence of a developing pattern is discernible in successive psalms even when their various authors were widely separated in time, such as those figuring in Book IV, which opens with the Prayer of Moses and closes with the Captivity (Psalms 90-106). Plainly a mighty Hand has been at work, a mighty Mind has designed the whole. The portrait that He limned was that of the Son of Man, the Christ of God.

☆　　　☆　　　☆

George Herne, Bishop of Norwich. *Psalms, Introduction and commentary.*
Dr. Lightfoot. *Harmonizing of the Old Testament. Order of the Psalms.*
J.J.S. Perowne. *Psalms.* (Especially ch. 1: *The Lyric Poetry of the Hebrews*).
W. Alexander, Bishop of Derry. *The Witness of the Psalms to Christ.*
Rev. E. Simmons. *A Spiritual Commentary on the Psalms.*
W. Kay. *The Psalms Translated from the Hebrew.*
E.B. Samuel. *The Prophetic Character of the Psalms*
'An Oxford Graduate'. *Christ the Key of the Psalter.*
E.W. Bullinger. *The Chief Musician.*
Stacey Waddy. *Homes of the Psalms.*

'Christianus'. *The Christ of the Psalms.*
J.G. Bellett. *Meditations on the Psalms.*
A.F. Kirkpatrick. *The Theology of the Psalms.*
David Baron. *Types, Psalms and Prophecies.*
A.T. Schofield and G. Biddulph. *The Journeys of Jesus Christ.*
David Baron. *Ancient Scriptures and the Modern Jew.*
Rabbi Dr. A. Altmann. *Wherein I Glory.*
Dr. J.W. Thirtle. *The Titles of the Psalms.*
Bishop Lowth. *On the Psalms.*

THE PORTRAIT

THE PORTRAIT

On the whole, the marvellous collection of poetry we call the Book of Psalms is a collection of songs and prayers by various writers simply put together over the centuries. Neither author not subject decides their sequence, and they are not in chronological order of composition, for some of the psalms of David appear among those obviously coloured by the Exile in Babylon. But though they seem to have been brought together haphazardly, the reader should have in mind that the Holy Scriptures also rank as great art, and that an important part of every truly great literary work is its structure. so we may postulate that it was the intent of the Holy Spirit to include order in their final compagination.

Although the psalms seem to follow a pattern, divine inspiration as the Master Planner has been secretly at work and has imposed a developing design that binds single psalms into groups, groups into hidden sequence, and the Five Books into an epic account of matters stretching in unbroken continuity from Eternity to Eternity, just as does the Bible itself.

Now, the thread that connects this heterogeneous collection is not at once discernible, but a clue is to be found in the general rule that in every great literary work of which human experience is the main theme, a preliminary sketch of the principle character may be expected in the opening scene or chapter. This is found in PSALM 1.

☆　　　☆　　　☆

PSALM 1.–

The First Psalm opens with 'Blessed is the man —' a blessing which at first appears to be addressed to all men who read, meditate and delight in the Law of the Lord, and indeed there is a blessing in so doing. But on the premise that a single plan binds the whole, the First Psalm must be understood as not merely an introduction to the work but an integral and vital part of it. It is therefore more than a general statement. It is the initial presentation of THE Man, the Blessed and Upright Man. As part of a divinely planned structure, the function of the First Psalm is not merely to depict a human ideal. It must portray God's Ideal Man, the Man in whom He was well pleased.

Here, then, is the opening chord of the great symphony which follows. It presents the identifying characteristics of Him of whom the Psalms will speak. It is the tonic note to which all the rest will be related, the basis on which the whole is to be constructed, by reference to which all later details must be gauged. Let us then contemplate the Portrait which is placed in so significant a prominence.

The First Psalm defines and portrays this Blessed Man — He walketh not in the counsel of the ungodly, nor standeth in the way of sinners, nor sitteth in the seat of the scornful. But these are only the negative aspects. His most recognisable feature, the one by which he is identified is the positive one: that his delight is in the Law of the Lord and in His Law doth he meditate day and night. This is the hall-mark. By this His character can be traced throughout the Book of Psalms. He is the one who can claim that 'I have walked in mine integrity' in Psalm 26; he is the Upright Man of Psalm 15 that worketh righteousness, and the Man who in Psalm 18 can assert that he has 'kept the ways of the Lord . . . All His judgments are before me, and . . . His statutes'. His enjoyment of the Law of the Lord is described in Psalm 19, and He is the Meditating Man of Psalm 119. cf. Vs. 97-104. He is the Righteous Man whose mouth speaketh wisdom, the Law of his God is in his heart; the Perfect Man whose end is peace. (Psalm 37). And so throughout all the psalms, the characteristics presented in the First Psalm trace a bright trajectory like luminous golden footprints pointing

His journey through time. He obeyed the injunction both of Moses and of Proverbs 6:21-23 — to 'love the Lord thy God, and keep his charge, and his statutes, and his judgments, and his commandments, always . . . and lay up these words in your heart and in your soul.'. (Deut. 11:1,18). Throughout His life Jesus' obedience and delight in the Law of the Lord proved the truth of this psalm's definition of Him, and His Identity through the psalms is revealed by reference to this feature outlined at the commencement. Meditation in the Law of the Lord reached in the Lord Jesus the fullness described and commanded by Moses —' . . . Diligently teach, talk of them when thou sittest in thine house, and when thou walkest by the way, and when thou liest down, and when thou risest up' . . . (Deut. 6:7,8).

The two verses which form the central part of this psalm and now follow, consist of a prolonged simile. In a masterpiece of this calibre a figure of speech has a pertinence to the whole and is not merely decorative. It should contain the germ of what is gradually to be revealed by the whole, expanding throughout the work as an oak grows from an acorn.

What, then, may be learnt of Him through this simile? It is not merely that He is 'like a tree'. This Perfect Man's similitude is that of 'a tree *planted by rivers of water* that bringeth forth his fruit in his season; his leaf also shall not wither; and whatsoever he doeth shall prosper', — or, come to fruition. The simile is that of luxuriant growth, perennial freshness and fullness of life without end. Such a tree is the Tree of Life planted by the pure river of water of life that proceeds out of the throne of God, seen by John (Rev. 22:2), whose leaves are for the healing of the nations. He is in Himself the fullness of Life: He is the Man who was Eternal Life in the flesh. The Tree of Life in Eden and the Pure River of Water of Life (Genesis to Revelation) were embodied physically and figuratively in Jesus. This Tree's rich and constant verdure knows no fading. He is the Blessed Man described by Jeremiah (17:8), like a tree planted by the waters, that shall not see when heat cometh and shall not be careful in the year of drought, neither shall cease from yielding fruit.

The world thought that He had 'withered' when, believing that He sought an earthly throne, they saw Him repudiated at last. In men's eyes it seemed that His leaf had faded when they succeeded in cutting Him down and He 'bare our sins in His own body on the tree' (I Pet. 2:24), but it was that we who were dead should live unto righteousness. This cutting down of that Tree was only temporary, so that His own eternal life might be given to them that believe (Gal. 3:22), and He was to spring into renewed life and still further fruitfulness for eternity.

An ungodly pretender to the throne would have been chaff driven away by the whirlwind, but this Tree of Life could not be done away. Having fulfilled the Eternal Father's will, He shared the Throne out of which there flows the River of Life for ever. In fact, those that thought themselves to be His executioners were actually carrying out on Him the means by which He should fulfil what God had designated from eternity that He should do — heal the nations.

The most prominent physical characteristic of this tree of Psalm I is its exuberant life. What effect will this perennial freshness have on Jesus' character and behaviour as a man? Such exuberance in human terms would denote perfect health and be expressed in abundant strength and unflagging energy. Combined with a fine intellect it would show eagerness and enthusiasm at work and hearty application in carrying out every task to perfection. In the Divine Man this burgeoning energy did not expend itself uselessly but was disciplined and under control.

On seeking in the Gospel narrative confirmation of this meaning of the simile of the Evergreen Tree we find it abundantly evident. Because of His vitality the Righteous One showed energy and determination, zeal, and a profound dedication to the fulfilment of His task, rejoicing at being the instrument to carry out the Father's eternal plan. Though He was to be rejected by the men He had come to save, it was for 'the *joy* that was set before Him' that He endured. (Heb. 12:2).

As He emerged from childhood His first recorded words were characteristic. They denoted His eagerness to begin the task which had been assigned Him: 'I must be about my

Father's business'. The words were spoken with the authority of adulthood; they reveal a wealth of previous thought about this business, and an intensity of devotion which, controlled and dedicated, was already channeled into this one purpose. He was eager to launch into it without delay.

His sense of mission was always very great: His consciousness of its uniqueness stimulated Him and elation must have filled His mind as He stepped forth into His public ministry to bring healing and the message of Eternal Life. In fact His work would eventually dismiss the angel with the flaming sword from the gates of Eden and make the Tree of Life available again to man.

He consecrated His life to this goal with earnestness and zeal as may be detected in such expressions as, 'For this cause I was born'; 'For this cause came I —'; 'Let us go into the next towns, that I may preach there also: for therefore came I forth'; and with urgency: 'I must work while it is day: the night cometh . . .' and so on. The frequent use in Mark's Gospel of the words 'straightway', 'immediately', and 'forthwith' show the same. He is portrayed in that Gospel as imbued with a purposeful spirit directed intensely to the fulfilling of His missionary task: eager, industrious, untiring, He gave Himself unstintingly; plunging heartily and enthusiastically into the work His Father had appointed for Him. He came up from the waters of baptism 'full of the Spirit', and after the Temptation He 'returned in the power of the Spirit' to Galilee, where 'His word was with power' and men marvelled. This is exactly the counterpart in human terms of the tree simile of Psalm One.

This was the effect of His being the Tree planted by rivers of water, drawing His energy from the Source of Life. Aware of the fact that the main purpose of His human life was His sacrificial death, He was also alive to the fact that by His life, His teaching, His example, He had a mission to fulfil before His death and apart from it. He had to show the Father. He had to teach the Divine view of the Law and show how the Law had been circumscribed, perverted and 'made of none effect' by the traditions of men. (Mat. 15:6-9). He had to clear away the tangled undergrowth that

27

choked and obscured the truth; He had to choose and instruct a certain few, His disciples, to carry on the work. He had to open their eyes to the new dimension of 'God with us', and form the 'new bottles' to hold the 'new wine' of His teaching. There was a great deal to be done and He must have been exuberant with the joy of having it to do.

He said 'As the Father hath life in Himself, so hath He given to the Son to have life in Himself' (John 5:26). In other psalms we get a hint of the vista which Jesus inwardly contemplated, of the life which through the mediation of His sacrifice would be given to man, life which would be 'length of days for ever and ever' (Psa. 21). The eternal life which he enjoyed would be shared with men, with all who accepted the leaves of His healing. When it came to showing His sincere desire to bring benefits to man — not material prosperity but life everlasting — the intensity of His love was expressed literally in His *Passion*.

As one senses the fullness of life in the Just Man who is likened to the tree planted by rivers of water one realizes that Psalm 1 is placed at the outset because it outlines the character of Him of Whom the Psalms are to be a spiritual biography and portrait. The righteous man of Psalm 1 is none other than 'Jesus Christ the Righteous'. (I John 2:1).

☆   ☆   ☆

PSALM 2.

Opening with the question, 'Why do the heathen rage?' this psalm is a document formally and plainly presenting the origin of the claims and rights of the Son of God. It states the source of His entity and of His powers. At the same time it affirms the identity of the First Person used throughout this and all the psalms that follow: 'The Lord hath said unto me Thou art my son; this day have I begotten thee.' (v. 7) This is the only statement given to men about the fact that took place in eternity long before the Creation and the beginning of time. But for this psalm we would not know that God had made this decree, just as but for the 40th Psalm we would never know how and why the Son offered Himself. Both events are beyond the ken of man and these ineffable decisions are revealed only in the Psalms.

Psalm 2 is the declaration and proclamation of the divine and royal lineage of the Righteous Man described in the first psalm.

> I have set my king upon my holy hill of Zion;
> I will declare the decree:
> The Lord said unto me, Thou art my son;
> This day have I begotten thee.

There follows the statement of the extent of his kingdom (v. 8) —

> Ask of me, and I shall give thee
> the heathen for thine inheritance
> and the uttermost parts of the earth
> for thy possesion.

It endows the Son with both authority and power (v. 9) —

> Thou shalt break them with a rod of iron.

It is therefore of no avail that 'the heathen rage'; the people 'imagine a vain thing' (v. 1) when they think they can break away from His rule (v. 3). The decree has gone forth from Him who is Omnipotent and Supreme, who 'sitteth in the heavens', and who will laugh at their puny defiance (v. 4). The proclamation ends by counselling the kings of the earth to be wise and present their submission to Him, that they be not destroyed. Their trust will bring them not servitude but blessing; their defiance will cause them to perish. The Everlasting Father issued the decree of the Sonship, and Omnipotence publishes the proclamation of his absolute sway. The warning is added: Be wise now, therefore, O ye kings; ... Kiss the Son, lest He (the Omnipotent) be angry. (11,12). 'Ye do well to take heed', says Peter (II Pet. 1:19).

Now if we examine the structure of this psalm we shall find out who speaks the words and thus shall learn by what authority men are counselled to submit and pay their homage.

Verses 1-5 are spoken, ostensibly, by the psalmist —

> The kings of the earth set themselves,
> > and the rulers take counsel together,
> Against the Lord and against His Anointed . . . (v. 1,2).

But this speaker is shown to be more than a man, because he knows:

a) men's thoughts and imaginings; their secret plans; their secret defiance and rebellion. v. 1-3.

He also knows:

b) What happened in eternity past (the Investiture of the Son);
c) What happens in the heavens. v.4 (He that sitteth in the heavens shall laugh . . .)
d) The character of God. His derision and His anger. 4,5.

This speaker is aware of the *present* (the heathen rage . . .); and of the *future* (He shall deride, shall speak, shall vex them . . .). The person who knows this is not only historian but prophet. He is Divine. He knows all things. Yet He speaks of Him 'that sitteth in the heavens' in the 3rd. person. And He is not the same who says in v. 7 'The Lord said unto me, Thou art my son'. Thus it is evident that it is the Holy Spirit who is speaking. There are noticeably three Voices:

> v. 6 — *I* set *my* King, . . . *my* holy hill.
> v. 7 The Lord said unto *me*, *Thou* art my Son.

In v. 8 and 9 the Son tells that the Father said to Him; Ask of me . . . Thou shalt break . . .
Verse 10, 'Be wise now . .,' is not spoken by the Father because He is referred to in the 3rd. person, v. 11. It is not spoken by the Son because He is also referred to in the 3rd person, v. 12. Verses 10-12 are spoken by the same Speaker of the opening — 'lest *he* be angry', that is, the Lord, of whom he spoke in v. 11, 'Serve the Lord with fear . . .' Thus it becomes evident that the first 5 verses and the last three, which counsel the kings, are spoken by the Third Person of the Trinity to those that 'imagine a vain thing'.

The Son tells that when the Father made the decree, He authorized Him to ask and receive the heathen for His inheritance.

This answers the question of why God does not strike the wicked now. Jesus has asked for that inheritance and God's uplifted hand is withholding the stroke while the saving grace of the Son is working among the 'heathen', forming His inheritance. He started first with the heathen round about Israel: The Decapolis with the Gadarene man whom He healed; Phoenicia with the Syro-Phenecian woman; men came from Tyre and Sidon (Mark 3:8), from Greece; the Roman centurion received His help. He claimed the heathen 'for His inheritance' as gradually the kingdom spread to the 'uttermost parts of the earth', and one day He will make them His 'possession'. But this grace is only temporary. Therefore, says the Holy Counsellor: Pay your homage now to the Son lest the Almighty allow His anger to burst out upon you. The consequence of evil is a fact. This is not a threat but a prophecy. The wicked shall be destroyed.

There are the wicked; they shall perish. But there are also the blessed. v. 12, 'Blessed are they that put their trust in Him'. In this was manifested the love of God, says John (I John 4:9), because God sent His only-begotten Son into the world, that we might live through Him.

The framework of this psalm contains the whole panorama of God's eternal plan. God the Omnipotent will be, must be, obeyed. That is the setting. The whole universe owes Him obedience because He is supreme. Rebellion is treason, and treason carries the death penalty. But when He said, 'Thou art my Son', it was with the intent of winning men to Himself and to blessedness. The wicked are enjoined to serve the Lord with fear, that they be not destroyed. Their submission will bring them not servitude but blessing; their defiance will cause them to perish. The Everlasting Father issued the decree and gave the Son absolute sway.

Comparative passages in the Gospels are found at the baptism and the transfiguration of Jesus. 'Straightway coming up out of the water . . . there came a voice from heaven saying, Thou art my beloved Son, in whom I am well pleased.' (Mark 1:10,11). And at the Transfiguration men heard the voice out of the cloud say, 'This is my beloved Son, hear Him!' It was the cloud out of which the same Voice had issued the Commandments to Moses demanding obedience on pain of death.

Let us, in view of the similarity of these pronouncements and the proclamation in the Psalm, examine the account of the early days of Christ's public fulfilling of His commission as the Son.

From the Jordan and His baptism He came 'full of the Spirit' and was led by the Spirit into the wilderness. After the Temptation He returned 'in the power of the Spirit' into Galilee, where 'they were astonished at His doctrine, for His word was with power'. (Luke 4:1,14, 32). Then He entered the Synagogue and taught. (Mark 1:21). Hence His first act after His baptism and God's public avowal of Him as His Son was to go straight into the camp of the foe. He had come to destroy the power of evil and there, in the wilderness defying Satan, He affirmed His unswerving allegiance to the Law, to the Prophets, and to God as Supreme Head, and in addition declared war on the Evil One himself, by announcing Himself as 'the Lord thy God', not to be tempted. The invitation to 'fall down and worship' is rebutted with a sharp reminder to Satan of his own downfall and position of servitude — 'It is written, *thou shalt worship the Lord thy God, and Him only shalt thou serve!*' For Satan had had the effrontery to offer the Son what the Father had already promised Him, i.e. 'all the kingdoms of the world'. Satan's challenge to the Son's sway was met with the calm stern command to serve, and so he 'left Him for a season', but the conflict was to continue. Satan's further attacks would be aimed at snatching His earthly life from Him so that He should not carry out His redemptive task, and he further sought to hinder Him and His work by raising jealousy and anger in the hearts of the very men (Scribes and Pharisees) whose business it was to teach men about God.

The clash with the powers of evil was immediate. The unclean spirit was *in the synagogue*. When Jesus returned from the wilderness, back to the world of men, victorious over the Tempter and determined to carry out His mission of bringing God's message of love to mankind, He entered the place of worship. He had come to do good, to heal, to teach, but at the first opportunity of doing this He found that the devil was there, forestalling Him, lurking in the very place where God was worshipped.

Jesus must have known that the unclean spirit was in the synagogue, and by His entry there, challenged it. Until then it was hidden, secretly in ambush in the last place in the world where men would expect to find it, but challenged by the presence of the Master of the House, it was forced to cry out and discover itself. Jesus' supremacy over Satan, affirmed in the wilderness, here began to be manifest publicly. The evil spirit acknowledged Him — 'I know thee who Thou art, the Holy One of God'. (Mark 1:24). Jesus rebuked it, and it was obliged to obey and come out of the man, for Jesus had come from the wilderness the Victor. But the Scribes and Pharisees were far from pleased at this manifestation of the power of God in their midst. They asked, amazed and disconcerted, angry at the challenge to their own supremacy: 'What doctrine is this?' Later, when Jesus expounded it, announcing the mercy of God extended to those outside of Israel (as with the widow of Zarephath and Naaman the Syrian), 'they were filled with wrath and rose up and thrust Him out of the city, and led Him to the brow of the hill whereon their city was built, that they might cast Him down headlong.' (Luke 4:24-30).

We are not told by the Evangelist what His inner thoughts were at this treatment, but by linking the events in the early chapters of Mark and Luke with this psalm we may deduce them. Humanly speaking He could not have expected such a cold — such a violent — reception; not from men, at any rate, and certainly not from those who represented God to them. So we have in Psalm 2 the incredible fact of their violence, opposition and hatred; 'They set themselves against His anointed, saying Let us break asunder, let us cast away . . .' — headlong.

But, He would ruminate, theirs was not the last word. He, 'passing through the midst' of His would-be destroyers, 'went His way'. He escaped out of their hands, and would recall the words —

> He that sitteth in the heavens shall laugh;
> The Lord shall have them in derision.

Puny men, puny hatred. They could neither frustrate God's Will nor defeat His purpose. God would laugh at their efforts, for now His own beloved Son was on earth to carry out His plan of redemption, and the hand of man would be his instrument. Some day 'God shall speak unto them in His wrath, and vex them in his sore displeasure' (v. 4,5). Meanwhile, despite the worst that men could do, here He was, to do the Will of the Father, and He could hear God say — 'Yet have I set my king upon my holy hill of Zion'. First there would be the intervening hill called Calvary, but finally His feet shall stand on the holy hill of Zion as King (v. 6), and His eyes saw it as though it was already accomplished. The apostles also perceived the meaning of 'Why do the heathen rage?' when they met with violent opposition, though this was from Jewish authorities, for they quote the passage as spoken 'by the Holy Spirit through the lips of David thy servant'. (Acts 4:15,24).

Jesus' public declaration of His mission was made at its very outset — 'This day is this scripture fulfilled in your ears'. Not merely to bring deliverance to one poor man possessed of the evil spirit but that He was the expected and promised Messiah. THIS DAY — Tremendous concatenation of Eternity, Prophecy, and a moment in the Present!

May He not, at this time, have had in His mind the words of God's decree in psalm 2? And with solemn sternness, though unspoken, the words of warning that follow will have come to His memory when the mob was pushing him up to the brow of the hill to smash him on the rocks below, that the day would inevitably come when 'Thou shalt break them with a rod of iron: thou shalt *dash them* in pieces like a potter's vessel'. (v. 9). And his thoughts must have been those voiced by the psalmist —

Be wise, therefore, ye judges of the earth,
Serve the Lord with fear . . .
Kiss the Son lest He be angry and ye perish in the way.
(v. 9-12)

Meanwhile, 'Blessed are they that put their trust in God'.

☆   ☆   ☆

34

PSALM 3.—

'Lord how are they increased that trouble me!
Many are they that rise up against me!

Mark 3: 31-35. He was preaching on the shores of Lake Galilee, attracting crowds, healing all who came to Him. But His friends from Nazareth thought He had been carried away by a euphoria of zeal and enthusiasm, and they persuaded His mother and brothers to come and bring Him away from the jostling excited crowds. He was beside Himself, they said; it was improper that he should be mobbed by this rabble! So here they come to lead Him away, back to His home, where His family could restrain His exuberance. He was always so compassionate, His mother would be thinking, people would take advantage of His goodness. He could not be left there at their mercy. Look at the turmoil they had made already! Many were gathering together, insomuch that there was no room to receive them, no, not so much as about the door. And the multitude cometh together again, so that they could not so much as eat bread. So his mother was brought there to rescue Him. And so, more subtly, the enemy sought to silence Him.

His friends tried to restrain Him. His family wished to shield Him but now He realized that He must renounce even their love. He had left His Heavenly position in the bosom of the Father, He had left the Father's side. Then He had left His beloved earthly abode with its gentle simple comforts and the companionship of His godly mother and probably that of a loved younger brother (James). He had addressed Himself to the business on earth of God His Heavenly Father and taken to the dusty road, willing to bear the privations of an itinerant preacher so that His message might go abroad.

Instead of the cool shady courtyard of His home in Nazareth he had the hot dust of the roadways and nowhere to lay His head. In place of the godly discourse and quiet culture of His family he had the raucous cries and the jostling of the greedy crowds, many of them diseased and filthy. He had come from a family, who in spite of their enforced simplicity, were conscious of their great tradition and lived in the quiet dignity of the knowledge that they came of the royal line leading in direct descent from the great David, themselves the rightful royalty of their nation. Yet now He consorted with the commonest people and allowed the diseased of the whole region, many of them beggars, to come near, press upon Him, demand of His goodness more and still more. They were crowding in, eager to grasp this opportunity of free healing, and now His friends, concerned lest harm come to Him, have brought His mother all the way from Nazareth to ask Him to stop and come home. This behaviour was not only undignified, they would reason; it was dangerous! They would have both the priests and the military authorities like hornets about their ears if He went on!

Yet now see it from His viewpoint. He was full of the zeal of carrying out the mission entrusted to Him, fulfilling the Father's command with all diligence and with all His strength; earnestly, eagerly throwing Himself into His labour of love, unstintingly giving Himself out. His only link with His quiet earthly home was His mother who was still living there. Now she was to add her persuasion to that of His friends who knew that He had always been 'subject to' His earthly guardians. But He could not meet her. The moment had come when He must cast off even that bond and loosen the last tie. He must renounce His allegiance and obedience to His mother because His Father's business was urgent. The temptation to take the easier way had now come in crueller form, and He recognized it as such. In a flash His decision was made and He remained outwardly firm. With the anguish of farewell in His heart He said, 'Who is my mother?' — which meant (and still does, in the local idiom), 'I have no mother'; or, 'I have renounced her that was my mother'.

What went on in His mind during this time? Let us look at Psalm 3.

> Lord, how are they increased that trouble me! . . .
> Many are they which say of my soul,
> There is no help for Him in God. (v. 1,2).

That is what they had said: He is beside Himself. He is

36

not responsible for His actions. He needs to be taken care of. 'Selah' follows as He contemplates the irony of their statement. They said He was mad. Madness? He was bringing concord to poor tortured minds! The learned scribes said He was possessed of an unclean spirit (or was demented). So now even His friends and family seek to lay hold on Him. But in His mind the psalm goes on —

> Thou, O Lord, art a shield for me, my glory and
> lifter up of my head;
> I will not be afraid of ten thousands of people
> that have set themselves against me round about.

His heart communes with His God and He calls to Him to silence His enemies (v. 7). God did 'break the teeth of the ungodly', for how could they complain openly that He was doing too much good and healing too lavishly? By renouncing His family ties He had won the right to continue His work amid the turmoil of the needy, and as He thinks triumphantly of all those whom He had healed returning to their homes, He cries (v. 8) —

> Salvation belongeth to the Lord;
> Thy blessing is upon Thy people.

And silently with the Selah His mind goes over the day's work. He had made a determined start. With the help of God He would go on, forging His way to the winning for men that salvation which is of the Lord, and which He had been sent to proclaim.

PSALM 4.—

The first days and weeks of His ministry. Mark ch. 4 and 5.

Summing these up once again: Jesus had come from His baptism and open commitment to the preaching of John, sanctified before the multitude on the banks of the Jordan by the very voice of God from heaven ratifying what He was later to claim, clothed with the Holy Spirit Who had descended upon Him visibly, to fulfil His life's work. Holy zeal fills His mind and heart. What a soul to go and meet the rabble! He was buoyant with the new joy of being at last the bearer of God's good news to as many as would listen.

He soon found the needy crowd around Him, expectant, hopeful, joyously telling far and wide that healing came bountifully from His hands. They came (Mark 3:7,8) from all the country round about. He could not go to all of them but they flocked to Him. From Galilee and Judea, from Jerusalem and from Idumea, from the Mediterranean coast round Tyre and Sidon, they came to Him on the lake shores of Galilee.

They crowded round and pressed about Him until He and His disciples 'could not so much as eat bread', Mark writes. But there were also those that dissented, who were angry, and were moved only to thoughts of murder, to destroy Him. (Mark 3:6). He was grieved at the hardness of the Pharisees' hearts when in the synagogue they narrowly watched to see if He would heal the withered hand on the sabbath. But He healed it and it was 'restored whole as the other'.

This was not what the Pharisees wanted at all. They 'went forth and straightway took counsel with the Herodians (whom they disliked) against Him, how they might destroy Him'. (3:6). Then, later, when they saw the crowds flocking to Him, and He satisfying their demands, pleased that they came, no doubt, and healing them no matter how many, they thought Him mad. Perhaps He was, humanly speaking, 'beside himself' with the joy of being free to reach so many and say 'Be whole' to those broken by His arch-enemy Satan. It was His way of declaring the supremacy of God. Disease, the work of Satan, was healed by the hand of the Son. He did not spare Himself, but worked on hour after hour until after sundown.

But word reached Jerusalem and the scribes came north post haste to inquire into the furore, fearful of the consequences. He hath Beelzebub, they said, and by the prince of devils He casteth out devils. It was not so much an accusation as their only explanation, for their hard cold hearts had long ceased to contemplate the goodness and compassion of God and had only observed the hard impositions of the thousand petty laws laid down by men upon their religion by their traditions: a self-righteous dogma, not a spiritual understanding of Divine love. The only supernatural activity they had seen for many a decade was that of devil possession. So they ascribed the marvellous acts of healing to a super-demon possession, that of 'Beelzebub, prince of devils'.

Jesus explained patiently to these doctors of the law, and, true Teacher that He was, He gave them an incontrovertible argument with a simple illustration: How can Satan cast out Satan? If a kingdom is divided against itself, that kingdom cannot stand. (Mark 3:23-30).

But in His heart He knew that the victory over Satan's temptings in the wilderness had not been the final overthrow of His enemy. He knew that would not come until He could purchase man back to God with His own blood. He knew Satan's determination to hold fast his sway over men's hearts; He knew that Satan would pertinaciously attempt to obstruct His mission and bring it to naught, frustrate Him, even kill Him, for had He not declared open war and challenged Satan's power over the kingdoms of the earth?

Now as He goes forth He makes straight for the very territory where the enemy is king and assails the outposts; the hearts and minds of men subject to evil. Having overcome the violence of the Temptation in the wilderness and the gentleness of His mother's loving petition to return home; having committed Himself entirely to His Father's business and cast off every tie of blood or friendship, He addresses Himself to the combat with undeviating directness, serene in the strength of His confidence that God was with Him.

The cry in His heart at this time must have been Psalm 4:2 —

> O ye sons of men, how long will ye turn my glory into shame?
> How long will ye love vanity and seek after leasing? Selah.

His goodness attributed to Beelzebub! Turning His glory

into shame.

But their criticism of Him and condemnation of His procedure could not alter the fact that He was the godly Man of Psalm 1 who was like a tree planted by rivers of water. With confidence and comfort to Himself He would remember —

> Know that the Lord hath set apart Him that is godly
> for Himself
> The Lord will hear when I call unto Him. (Psa. 4:3).

God would give Him strength and wisdom for the task.

As there flashed before His mind's eye the many joyful faces and grateful hearts that had received His bounty, the many broken lives made whole again, He would think of the comparison in the psalm:

> There are many that say, Who will show us any good?
> Lord, lift up the light of Thy countenance upon us.
> Thou hast put gladness in my heart,
> More than in the time that their corn and their wine
> increased.

Did He here remember some joyous harvest celebration at the Feast of Weeks, when the corn and wine had been specially plentiful? How glad the people had been! They had danced and sung joyously for God's provision. The analogy suggests itself: This was the beginning of His harvest of Joy. Weary He was, but —

> I will both lay me down in peace, and sleep,
> For Thou, O Lord, only makest me to dwell
> in safety. (v. 8)

God would not let them destroy Him before time. He prays for the blessed light of God's countenance to be lifted upon Him, that is, that He might receive the priestly benediction, and in that power He will go forward serenely to His task.

The same verse will have come to Him again shortly afterwards, for He lay down in peace and slept in the poop of the fishing-boat as it was tossed roughly about in the Satanically raised storm. Meanwhile, He reviews the situation as it stands so far, in the parable of the Sower, and explains it to the disciples. He was scattering the good seed, but only a part of it fell on good soil. Thus He pictured Himself sowing far and wide and He knew that in spite of disappointments. His message would eventually be like the grain of mustard-seed that 'groweth up and becometh greater than all herbs'.

Then He said, Let us pass over unto the other side. He had been preaching, teaching, and healing on the shore of Galilee. Now He would go to 'the heathen'.

Did He know that the man with the legion of devils was immediately across on the other side? It was surely no chance that led Him there, for He re-crossed the lake the next evening. His mission across the sea was specifically to meet and heal that demoniac. Perhaps His ear had caught the sound of the poor madman's desparing cries. It may be that He went in calm defiance to storm that part of Satan's dominion, for the 'nations' were His for the asking, they were not the possession of the Rebel who claimed a right over them. The Father had said (2:8): Ask of me and I shall give thee the heathen for thine inheritance. Perhaps in the hours on the mountain top when He withdrew to pray all night, He was asking God the Father to give Him the heathen. So He said, 'Let us pass over to the other side'.

Satan exerted himself to stop Jesus from going, and to do away with Him if possible, for a great storm of wind rose in the night in the midst of the sea, and the waves beat into the ship. (Mark 4:37). The fishermen crew knew the Sea of Galilee well; they were expert seamen and had braved many a storm as it drove up and down the valley of the Jordan and was cupped in the lake by the surrounding hills. But this storm seemed unusually violent. All their efforts to get through were in vain and the waves swamped the ship. They had done their utmost to serve their august Passenger but a destructive force prevented them from carrying out His wish as Satan fought to prevent Jesus from setting foot among the 'heathen' which the enemy held under his own sway. The tempest raged and water began to fill the boat. The Master must be wakened. Wakened! He was asleep through all this tumult!

True, He must have been weary from the continuous pressures upon Him; much 'virtue' had gone out from Him to the many hundreds who had sought His healing in the past few weeks. But his sleep meant more than the repairing of physical strength. It was the relaxation of total confidence that God would give Him, as he had asked, the heathen for his inheritance. He 'communed with his own heart upon his bed and was still' (v. 4). It was faith; it was peace that brought sleep. It was trust. It was certain knowledge.

'Master, do you realize that we are in danger of drowning?' cried the disciples, waking Him in their anxiety, terrified at the fierce onslaught. Perhaps they wanted Him to be ready to jump for it when the ship should founder; perhaps they had faith that He could save the ship and bring them through the storm. But they did not expect Him to *stop the storm*!

He arose. He said, 'Peace, be still!' and there was a great calm. Then He asked, 'Why were you so afraid? Have you no faith?' They may well have thought to themselves that they had never seen the like of that before. Astonished, they asked each other what kind of man this was, whom the winds and waves obeyed.

But the fact remained that Satan's worst had been futile. He had been defeated again. He had tried to swallow up God's Messenger ('Christ' means 'the Sent One') in the elements of His own creation. But God was on the throne and Jesus was His Son, co-Creator with Him of all things. How could the sea have done other than obey His command of Peace and stillness?

So they reached the other side in the morning. There lay the shore, wet after the night's storm, but it would not in His eyes be sparkling with freshness in the early light. This was the country of the Gadarenes and the first sight that met Him was one of death and madness, the graveyard and the poor maniac He had come to heal. Dementia, tombs, and desolation, but He had come with a message of hope and life.

Perhaps he wanted a messenger to go for him, a telling witness to the power of God, to spread among the 'heathen' the message of healing and salvation. In order to commission this messenger He had to do more than cross the sea. He had to enter the preserves of Satan's dominion, and he directs His steps to the Gadarene maniac in whom two thousand demons have made their abode. On all sides He read the signs of thraldom to Satan. There were the tombstones; it is the place of corruption and death. There on the hillside were not sheep but swine. This is Satan's habitation. This is the effect of his rule: disease, decay, raving madness, demon possession, shrieks, violence, swine, uncleanness and death. And *His* thoughts had first been spoken to man in the cool of the evening among the trees of a garden when He communed with Adam as a friend! But since the sad evening when His voice was heard calling, 'Adam, where art thou?' that sweet communion had been broken and man had been 'afraid' ever since. Estrangement has led to violence and the rage of madness.

But see with what high courage Jesus goes into the enemy's camp and breaks into his very stronghold. 'Immediately there met Him out of the tombs a man with an unclean spirit'. The fetters and chains with which men had tried to subdue him had broken in pieces, and 'always, night and day, he was in the mountains and in the tombs, crying, and cutting himself with stones.' Had this any connection with the heathen custom in the worship of Baal, as when Elijah defied them on Carmel and they cried, 'Baal, hear us', and cut themselves till the blood ran? Perhaps that maniac's cries and self injury were a despairing appeal to God for help. If so, the divine ear had caught the imploring accents, and here He was.

He had just stepped ashore when this fierce creature espied Him from afar and, rushing headlong at Him, he fell at Jesus' feet and worshipped Him. God had sent His Answer to man's cry. But the demons did not wish for His help. For them He was an intruder. They make the man scream and rave: 'I adjure Thee by God that Thou torment me not!'

Jesus the Man was walking on the tangible earth but His Spirit strode in another realm, that of the principalities and powers of the air described by Paul to the Ephesians. It was in the world of the spirit where the real war was to be waged. The demons immediately recognize Him, as did the one in the synagogue at Capernaum, and proclaim His identity. 'Jesus, Thou Son of the most High God!' They even threaten Him by their superiority of numbers — 'We are legion'. Thus the poor man's mouth cries.

But with the sublime calm that had stayed the storm and with majestic mien Jesus commands them to come out of him. Now they are suppliant: they beg leave to go into the bodies of the swine. Of course they would, for that was the symbol of the defiance. Jesus sees how to make an end of both the evil spirits and unclean animals together, and gives leave, knowing what they evidently did not, that the terrified maddened beasts would rush headlong down the cliff and drown in the sea.

Yet see the reaction of the Gadarenes! This Man is coming over to impose His Jewishness upon us! Let Him go back over the border to His own country and keep to His own people. Healed the madman? What of it? He has destroyed our living! Get out!

Jesus' mission there was almost done, so their rejection of Him did not matter. The man was seated now at His feet, clothed and in his right mind. When Jesus turned to go back across the sea the poor grateful creature prayed to be allowed to follow Him and be His disciple. But Jesus needed a messenger to go among the Gadarenes and He gently commissioned the healed man to go back and tell what God had done for him. His words to this man might have been —

> Offer the sacrifice of righteousness
> And put your trust in the Lord. (v. 5).

The man's gratitude and worship were so sincere that he was willing to forego the happiness of following the Master who had freed him, and turning, he went back to the place of the swine and the tombstones; back to the world held under the sway of the evil one; and preached far and wide the liberation of grace. With determination and courage he travelled the whole region untiringly, to one city after another until he had preached Jesus to all the ten cities of the Decapolis.

And Jesus must have smiled to Himself at the discomfiture of Satan as He sailed back across Galilee to His own country that same day, for He had set foot in the domain of His inheritance — the heathen; His ambassadors would do the rest and He could say to God:

> Thou hast put gladness in my heart, more than in the
> time that their corn and their wine increased.
> I will both lay me down in peace and sleep, for Thou,
> Lord only makest me to dwell in safety. (4:7,8).

☆   ☆   ☆

PSALMS 5-10.

If we hold to our surmise that the Psalms contain a picture of Jesus' thoughts, if not a record of them, we find a very moving account indeed of the Anointed One's unspoken thoughts during the first weeks, perhaps months, of His public life. No doubt other psalms also express the feelings of this period, but for the sake of orderliness in our exploration let us suppose that the experiences in the early Psalms come in the same order as the narration in the gospel of Mark. We find a portrait of a highly sensitive and refined spirit courageously carrying out a duty entrusted to Him. It is a point of honour with Him not to flag but to go straight on and fulfill the purpose for which He came.

The next group of Psalms (5 to 10) suggests that as He entered further into this task it was with sensitivity amounting almost to a natural shrinking from the coarseness of the rebuffs. Each rough word, each horrible accusation, came as a blow almost physically felt. The ugliness of the religious leaders' animosity must have caused shock that set off vibrations in His nervous system very painful to bear. His face and manner remained composed, but inside He was weeping. Already His heart was wounded with a cruel hurt. This was the Man of Sorrows that the Prophet saw. Not only were the hearts of the leaders of the people hardened, but His good was evil spoken of. The night must have seen His tears often as He wept at the harsh

45

misunderstanding and wilful misinterpretation of His good will; wept at how far from love and compassion they had wandered and at how fixed in their evil ways they had become; wept because He had to limit His benefits to the few who came to Him for them.

The Psalms called 'Imprecatory' now take on a different meaning. They do not so much express curses as the poignant factor in His mind that spurred Him on. 'The wicked shall be cast into hell'. And He was on earth to offer God's hand of friendship and reconciliation to those who would turn to Him. Let us examine these psalms.

☆　　☆　　☆

PSALM 5:- (and Mark 6:1-30).

This psalm is a prayer such as Jesus might have prayed when He withdrew to the mountain top at night to gather strength for the day:

Give ear to my words, O Lord, consider my meditation.
Hearken unto the voice of my cry, my King and my God:
For unto Thee will I pray.
My voice shalt Thou hear in the morning, O Lord;
In the morning wil I direct my prayer unto Thee
And will look up. (vs. 1-3).

He prays for guidance —

Lead me, O Lord, in thy righteousness because of
mine enemies;
Make Thy way straight before my face.

He remembers the lying accusations of the Scribes and Pharisees:

There is no faithfulness in their mouth;
Their inward part is very wickedness,
Their throat is an open sepulchre,
They flatter with their tongue — (v. 9).

46

while their hearts are planning murder. The blind followers of a cold and formal religious ritual could not see what He could see, that their words were the 'noisome exhalations of a putrid heart' (Bishop Horne). His indignation at those leaders' perversion of the word of the Holy God can be gauged in the verse that follows:

Destroy Thou them, O God; let them fall by their own counsels
Cast Thou them out in the multitude of their transgressions;
For they have rebelled against Thee. (v. 10).

Here is the clue to the understanding of these imprecations. They are not expressions of anger and vengeance for personal insults received, but the statement of the just reward for rebellion against God. They are the 'workers of iniquity' whom the Lord abhors and will destroy. (vs. 5,6). In these imprecatory psalms we shall always find that reason given. Men's rebellion against God classifies them as participators in the satanic rebellion against the divine authority. To Jesus, as the Evangelist records, the distortion of the image of God by the self-righteous teachers of the people was the most terrible thing; they were faithless traitors, misrepresenting their God and King.

But as He contends in prayer, He rejoices with holy joy at the thought of those who, like Himself, love and trust God:

Let all those that put their trust in Thee rejoice:
Let them shout for joy . . . ;
Let them also that love Thy name rejoice in Thee.
For Thou, O Lord, wilt bless the righteous;
With favour wilt Thou compass him as with a shield.
(vs. 11,12).

He is the 'Righteous One', hence like Jeremiah, He need not fear the angry faces of His enemies, for His heart will be compassed about by God's shield. What a touching view of the Saviour in His humanity as we recognize in Him the same human needs as ourselves and observe how His prayer brought reassurance, strength and joy in the trial, thus blazing the way for every soul that avails itself of the same resource.

PSALM 6.

This is the cry of one whose 'soul is sore vexed'. He cries:

> Have mercy on me, O Lord, for I am weak;
> O Lord, heal me, for my bones are vexed. (v. 2)

After those first weeks of constant walking, teaching, contending with the detractors of His goodness, with no home to retire to for rest, He must at times have felt a great physical weariness. That Jesus could experience this feeling we are told in John 4: 'Jesus being wearied sat thus on the well.' It is a mistake to think of Him as untouched by human limitation of strength, for did He not 'bear our infirmities'? In this psalm He tells of His weariness of body. He felt exhausted, for He had spent Himself beyond human strength. For days on end He had not had proper meals, had hardly even slept as hour after hour needy ones pressed upon Him and crowds gathered, each demanding something of Him. His nights were spent in prayer. He had given Himself out, fed them with Himself, the Bread of Life. Now He was experiencing the effect on His overtaxed human frame. 'My soul is sore vexed', perhaps thinking of the fury and threatening insults of those who posed as holy men; thinking also of the poor broken bodies and minds that so harrowingly besought His help. What devastation had been wrought by God's foe! 'How long, O Lord?' He cries in anguish of spirit —

> For in death there is no remembrance of Thee;
> In the grave who shall give Thee thanks? (v. 5).

If He spares Himself, how will these people learn the truth about God's mercy and goodness? He must press on, urgently, for the time was so short. His agony of heart becomes acute.

I am weary with my groaning; all the night make I
　　my bed to swim; I water my couch with tears.
Mine eye is consumed because of grief; It waxeth
　　old because of all mine enemies. (v. 6,7).

So writes David, and the words picture the anguish of Jesus at the disbelief of those He had come to save.

Then His soul rises above the tide of weariness as its oneness with God asserts itself and He denounces them vigorously —

Depart from me, all ye workers of iniquity,
For the Lord hath heard the voice of my weeping.
The Lord hath heard my supplication;
The Lord will receive my prayer. (vs. 8,9).

Let all mine enemies be ashamed and sore vexed;
Let them return and be ashamed suddenly. (v. 10).

When His mission is accomplished they will be put to shame, and in the assurance of faith He takes His rest. The certainty of ultimate victory and the vindication of all His claims is the undercurrent of the psalms of imprecation. We may gather from this one that many a night was spent not only in sweet communion with the Father but with anguish and tears as He 'groaned in the spirit and was troubled'. (John 11:33).

☆　　　☆　　　☆

PSALM 7.

Here are expressed the thoughts of a man who has been misinterpreted and cruelly rebuffed but who knows his heart is pure in God's sight.

If I have rewarded evil unto him that was at
　　peace with me;
(Yea, I have delivered him that without cause was
　　mine enemy);

Let the enemy persecute my soul and take it;
Yea, let him tread down my life upon the earth,
and lay mine honour in the dust. (vs. 4,5).

Like Job's claim, followed by a similar oath (Job 31), this is a vehement statement of innocence against an unjust accusation. Such could have been the response of Jesus at the onslaught of His opponents, the religious leaders who hated His simplicity of approach. He cries to God —

Deliver me, lest he tear my soul like a lion,
Rending it in pieces . . . (v. 2).

(Note that both the simile and the singular pronoun 'he' are significant here). It is the arch-enemy who is the instigator of their vile intimations. (Mark 3:22; and ch. 7). His indignation at the affront that these wicked men should attribute to Beelzebub the goodness of God and His power is expressed in the cry:

Arise, O Lord, in thine anger; lift up Thyself
because of mine enemies. (6).

He lays His heart open to God's scrutiny and prays (v. 8) —

Judge me, O Lord, according to my righteousness,
And according to my integrity that is in me —

Only the Son of God could say 'I do always those things that please Him (God)' (John 8:29) Only Christ dare offer Himself to God's judgment by the standard of His own integrity.

He prays that wickedness may come to an end and the just be established (v. 9), and adds, confident in His affirmation, 'My defence is of God, which saveth the upright'. It is the hallmark by which the Speaker may be identified: He is the Righteous Man of Psalm 1, whose thoughts now pass on to the destiny awaiting those evil doers. In His wrath, God will 'whet his sword; He will bend His bow and make it ready' (v. 12). Perhaps the imagery is from Moses' song in Deut. 32:41 —

> If I (God) whet my glittering sword and mine hand take
> hold on judgement, I will render vengeance to mine
> enemies and reward them that hate me.

He thinks how the evil of the rebellious will return on
their own head:

> He made a pit, and digged it, and is fallen into the
> ditch which he made. (v. 15).

The full meaning of this statement was fulfilled when the
title 'King of the Jews' was placed above the Cross of Jesus.
Those who reject God's message of love will have neither
excuse nor escape. The concluding words are of praise and
joy through faith:

> I will praise the Lord according to His righteousness;
> And I will sing praise to the name of the Lord most high.
> (v. 1).

Thus Jesus' spirit remained buoyant and His mind serene
as He prepared to face the tumult and the opposition no
matter how violent. How well this feature of joy fits in with
Jesus's own words recorded by John (15:11) — 'These
things have I spoken unto you that *my joy* might remain in
you, and that *your joy* might be full'. This holy joy in the
midst of the most adverse circumstances was the astonishing
key-note of His human existence.

PSALM 8.

This lovely pastoral poem could express the thoughts of
Jesus as He walked down from the hill-top of communion
and refreshment in the early morning after His vigil. The
whole sweep of the skies had been above Him, starred, all
night. He had watched their bright movement across the

firmament and now at dawn He would see the clear arch of blue overhead and beyond, with perhaps some white clouds blowing high over the valley; the hillside probably terraced by husbandmen, the rich soil at the foot of the hill giving nourishment to small, carefully cultivated farms in the vale below. He would see life awakening as He came down in the early dew, and His heart would rise in joy and praise as the first rays of sunlight cast their golden blessing on the new day. It was not until He could look on these things with the eyes of humanity that He would be moved by their beauty and sense the marvel of it. Creation speaks to men of the presence of God, and so also it would to the eyes of Jesus:

> O Lord our Lord, how excellent is Thy name in
>   all the earth!
> Who hast set Thy glory above the heavens . . .
>
> When I consider the heavens, the work of Thy
>   fingers,
> The moon and the stars, which Thou hast ordained;
> What is man that Thou art mindful of him?
> And the son of man that Thou visitest him? . . .
>
> For Thou hast made him a little lower than the angels
> And hast crowned him with glory and honour. . . .
>
> Thou madest him to have dominion over the works
>   of Thy hands
> Thou hast put all things under his feet.

David's admiration is for the condescension of God towards human beings but the Epistle to the Hebrews authorizes us (2:7-9) to address these words to God about Jesus. Yet we see the human appraisal of God's mercy and goodness to every man, also. Here in the Second Adam's appreciation of the marvels of God's creation in its purity and wonder but His heart's perfect obedience would enable Him to see the beauties of earth from the standpoint of man before the fall. Besides, this fair land was peculiarly His own, through God's promise to Abraham and His own descent from David.

As His heart revels in the view spread out before Him, the living creatures too are noticed —

All sheep and oxen, yea, the beasts of the field — perhaps dotted about the valley, starting their day's work; others are suggested too: The fowl of the air, and the fish of the sea — perhaps He could look across to the Mediterranean or to Galilee — and He returns to the opening exclamation:

> O Lord, our Lord, how excellent is Thy name
> in all the earth!

It is as though the human Jesus' contemplation of the beauty and marvels of nature caused Him to echo the words spoken at the Creation (Gen. 1:12,25,28,etc.) — 'And God saw that it was very good'. He had been there with God when they were created. (Prov. 8:25-31).

Note: 'From the hilltop behind the town of Nazareth, the whole land from Hermon to Samaria, and from the Great Sea to Idumea and Decapolis beyond Jordan, lay spread out like a map'.

> The Journeys of Jesus Christ the Son
> of God'. A.T. Schofield and
> G. Biddulph

☆   ☆   ☆

PSALM 9.

Here is a psalm of praise for the other marvellous though less tangible works of God. His enemies are turned back, they fall and perish at His presence (v. 3), destructions come to a perpetual end (6), judgment will be administered in uprightness (8), He will be a refuge for the oppressed (9), the wicked shall be turned into hell (17). This picture of the kingdom age when God's Chosen One shall reign in justice suggests, by its early place in the progress of the Messiah that in God's eyes that reign was inaugurated when Jesus entered upon His public life on earth. There are hints, surprising in this context, of His coming power, of His sufferings and death (v. 13), resurrection (14), and victory (15,16). But the main theme of the psalm is praise. The 'first person' of the song joyfully proclaims His praise to the Most High, recounts the motives for this, and looking beyond the present, sees the fulfilment of the purposes of God. The play on the tenses of the verbs throughout lends dramatic vividness and provides a glimpse into the divine workings of the 'timeless mind of Christ'. (See John 3:13) — 'The son of man which is in heaven'. He speaks of Himself as being 'in heaven' even when He was actually on earth.

The psalm ends with words which recall the shout of Moses as the Tabernacle moved forward on a new day's march (Num. 10:35):

> Arise, O Lord; let not man prevail. (v. 19).

It was also the exultant cry of David (Psalm 132:8) as the Ark of the Covenant was going up to the City of Zion!

The joy that must have filled the heart of Jesus as God's grace was manifested in spite of opposition thus early on, in the healing of the diseased and especially at the first raising back to life from the dead (the daughter of Jarius, Mark 5:22-43) is expressed here:

> I will be glad and rejoice in Thee:
> I will sing praise to Thy name, O Thou most high. (v. 2).

and His own inward shout of exultation at the start of the work which should give Him the victory over Death and Satan —

> O thou enemy, destructions are come to a perpetual end! (v. 6).

Luke tells of one such occasion of His rejoicing (Luke 10:21) — 'In that hour Jesus rejoiced in spirit, and said, I thank Thee, O Father, Lord of heaven and earth, that Thou hast hid these things from the wise and prudent and hast revealed them unto babes; even so, Father; for so it seemed good in Thy sight . . . And He turned Him unto His disciples and said privately, Blessed are the eyes which see the things which ye see: . . .' Thus Jesus showed that not only His heart rejoiced but He pointed out that there was also occasion for His disciples to rejoice with Him, this being a unique privilege. These psalms of rejoicing and thanksgiving must have found frequent and ready echo in

His mind, and it is lovely to think of the holy joy with which He envisioned the redemption of mankind, their deliverance from the power of evil, and the fulfilment of God's will that men should be saved. It is this vision of the ultimate overthrow of the enemy that keeps His eyes glad even as He beheld in man the ravages of sin, and His footsteps firm when a human nerve might have faltered at the ordeal He was to undergo.

He would think perhaps, as He started the early stages of His progress thither, of the Gadarene's labour of love and gratitude in witnessing to the regions beyond, for He calls upon all those whom He had healed to do this —

> Sing praises to the Lord which dwelleth in Zion:
> Declare among the people His doings. (vs. 10,11).

Go back and tell what great things God hath done for thee. Go and tell them that . . .

> He forgetteth not the cry of the humble. (v. 12).

The thought of how the demons had been sent to their destruction in the swine seems to return, and He rejoices that 'The heathen are sunk down in the pit that they made'. The metaphor of the 'net which they hid' in which 'their own foot is taken' must often have seemed apposite later when the Pharisees and Sadducees, the Scribes and Doctors of the Law, all set their wily traps for Him, and when even Pilate tried to make Him speak words of sedition — 'Art Thou a King, then?' To the first He brings the answers of His wisdom; to the last His reply is silence.

Because of the fearful end awaiting those who refuse to acknowledge God He prays that men may turn while yet there is the time —

> The Wicked shall be turned into hell . . .
> Put them in fear, O Lord, that the nations (heathen) may know themselves to be but men. Selah. (16-20).

☆   ☆   ☆

PSALM 10.

Here is a picture of men's behaviour as seen by holy eyes: They are given over to evil doing, boasting in their pride, persecuting the poor; blessing the covetous whom the Lord abhorreth; forgetting God's judgments; man's mouth is full of cursing, deceit and fraud; under his tongue is mischief and vanity.

The years spent at Nazareth were sweet quiet years in the society of His God-fearing family; perhaps apart from the Synagogue and the carpenter's shop He had had few dealings with the harshness of the outside world of bitterness, money-making, and of men treading each other down. He would know of it but be aloof from it. The catalogue here lists men's wickedness with all the horror with which He would now behold it. Its intensity conveys His astonishment and grief that this should be. Evil is found not only in the commerce of the city. It sits in the 'lurking places of the villages'; evil men lie in wait in the secret places to murder the innocent and their 'eyes are privily against the poor'. the wicked 'doth catch the poor . . . he croucheth and humbleth himself, that the poor may fall' into his net.

The graphic description suggests His indignation and anger that men have departed so far from God as to think that He cannot see their evil deeds —

He hath said in his heart, God hath forgotten;
He hideth His face; He will never see it . . . (v. 11).

During His ministry (Mark 7) Jesus named and de-nounced the hypocrisy, the emptiness and the harsh selfishness of priests and Pharisees, and gives a more biting and hideous catalogue than even the psalmist's — 'for from within, out of the heart of men, proceed evil thoughts, adulteries, fornications, murders, thefts, covetousness, wickedness, deceit, lasciviousness, an evil eye, blasphemy, pride, foolishness —'. How frightful was the sight as He, like Ezekiel of old, saw what was done in secret within the Temple walls and further, into the hearts of men. 'For Jesus knew . . .' John constantly reminds us.

56

He would pray in the words of this Psalm —

> Arise, O Lord God, lift up Thine hand; forget not
> the humble. (v. 12).

Thou hast seen it; for Thou beholdest mischief and spite
To requite it with Thine hand;
The poor committeth himself unto Thee;
Thou art the helper of the fatherless. (v. 14).

— the very ones whom He saw being robbed and oppressed
even then. Here we may understand why He should pray in
His righteous wrath:

> Break Thou the arms of the wicked and the evil man;
> Seek out his wickedness till Thou find none.

His mind then leaps forward, following its habitual trend,
to that blessed time of heaven on earth when 'The Lord is
King for ever', and the godless have 'perished out of the
land' (v. 16). Thus communing with Himself and with the
Father, He will press on and preach to men, for

> Thou wilt prepare their heart, Thou wilt cause Thine
> ear to hear — (17),

and the great day will dawn when 'the man of the earth'
may no more oppress. What kept His spirit buoyant in spite
of man's intemperance and inhumanity to his fellows was
the thought of that happy day when He should bring
righteous judgment to the earth.

PSALM 11.

The Lord Jesus found great solace in solitude. It must have
been particularly necessary during those first months of His
ministry. He resorted to the quietude of the hilltop to
commune with His Father. On several occasions it is

recorded that He withdrew from the town (cf John 12:36). The harsh sounds must have grated on Him, but His work would oblige Him to stay among the throngs —

How say ye to my soul. Flee as a bird to your mountain?

He must often have been sickened by the sight of how

the wicked make ready their arrow and bend their bow that they may privily shoot at the upright in heart.

The realization that this was done not exceptionally but was a universal behaviour must have come as a shock to Him, making Him long to go apart and enjoy the harmony between His spirit and the Father's.

The Psalm continues in words that Jesus might have used to encourage Himself. He must be strong, He must stay the course and exert Himself further to testify of the Father. He must brave the surrounding wickedness, for if He should flag, how shall man be saved? 'If the foundation be destroyed, what can the righteous do?' He must refresh Himself in retreat but return to the tumult, for

The Lord is in His holy temple, the Lord's throne
  is in heaven;
His eyes behold, His eyelids try, the children of men.
                                                    (v. 4).

The psalmist admits that the righteous are tried, but this is because God wishes to prove them; or, perhaps the meaning is singular, He Himself is being put to the test. But to the persistently wicked is reserved eternal punishment because they know the evil they do. They 'love violence' and must be destroyed, (v. 6) because

... the righteous Lord loveth righteousness
His contenance doth behold the upright.

The Son who had come from the Father's bosom knew the nature of God and was ever conscious of the light of the Father's countenance lifted up upon Him, giving peace.

☆   ☆   ☆

PSALM 12.

As Jesus observed on every hand the many signs of man's perversity, it must sometimes have seemed impossible that any impact would be made on their hardened hearts. The oppression he saw would have been bad enough if exercised by the Gentile conquerers and overlords, but it was infinitely worse coming from the Jews themselves upon their own people. In this psalm one senses dismay as He looked about Him, seeing this. 'Help, Lord!' He cries, 'for the godly man ceaseth and the faithful fail from among the children of men.' The ungodly not only oppress the poor but basely favour the rich; they flatter and are double-dealers. They are contemptuous of the law and say, 'Our lips are our own, who is Lord over us?' (v. 4). This might actually have happened when he reproved them of deceipt and greed, especially the proud Pharisees, to whom He said, 'Go ye and learn what that meaneth, I will have mercy and not sacrifice' (Mat. 9:13).

> For the sighing of the needy, now will I arise,
> saith the Lord (v. 5).

Or when He denounced the Scribes and Pharisees as hypocrites, who 'for a pretence make long prayers in public while you devour widows' houses . . . Hypocrites! Ye pay tithe of mint and anise and cummin, and have omitted the weightier matters of the law, judgment, mercy and faith.' (Mat. 23:13-33). To His admonitions they replied, 'Thou hast a devil!' (cf John 7:20; 8:48; 10:20; etc.).

God will have the last word.

> The words of the Lord are pure words,
> as silver tried in the furnace, purified seven times. (v. 6).

With what sweet relief Jesus would turn from the harsh retorts of 'this generation of vipers' (Mat. 23:33) to the pure silver sound of the Word of God!

☆   ☆   ☆

PSALM 13.

By continuing to explore the possible place of these psalms within the experience of our Lord on earth, we may find here an illustration of His spirit's quick rallying power and the resources He drew on when hard pressed, for in a few verses the tone changes from the anguished cry of —

How long wilt Thou forget me, O Lord?

to bold faith: My heart shall rejoice in Thy salvation, and praise: I will sing unto the Lord for He hath dealt bountifully with me (v. 5,6).

In the contrast of these moods there is coupled a suggestion of Jesus' true humanity and His true oneness with God. The sight of men flouting God's commands must have been horrifying to Him who had been with the Father where angels fly to do His bidding! It must have weighed heavily on His extraordinarily sensitive spirit to know as no mere human can know, how man's indifference pains and angers Almighty God. Yet through communion with Him the burden is lifted and He can sing God's bounty to Him.

Thus this psalm may be read as a plea of the Holy Son on earth to His Father in Heaven, whence a most touching possibility emerges. It would appear by placing it in this context, that Jesus felt very keenly the vulnerability of His human frame. His human life seems to be a period of exile in a land under thrall of the enemy. He prays.

O Lord my God: lighten mine eyes lest I sleep
the sleep of the death.

The 'enemy' (v. 2) being in the singular is surely the power of death (v. 3) and this casts light on the opening questions,

How long wilt Thou forget me, O Lord? For ever?
How long wilt Thou hide Thy face from me?

Did He foresee that while He was being made an offering for the world's sin, the Father would avert His face? This would be far worse than man's contempt, the infamy, or the physical suffering involved. How long would it last? For ever? Perhaps He wondered if it might be required of Him to remain a very long time without the light of God's countenance. Even the shortest space would seem an eternity of darkness. The thought was intolerable. It might be that it was at such a time that the Father answered His petition of 'How long?' with the words that Jesus later passed on to His disciples prophetically: 'For as Jonah was three days and three nights in the whale's belly, so shall the Son of man be three days and three nights in the heart of the earth.' (Matt. 12:40).

Continuing this train of thought, we hear Him pray most earnestly for the Resurrection: note the emphasis in the two verbs together:

> Consider and hear me, O Lord my God:
> Lighten mine eyes, lest I sleep the sleep of death. (v. 4);
> Lest mine enemy say, I have prevailed against him:
> And those that trouble me rejoice when I am moved.

He prays that God will bring Him back from the dominion of death into the light of His countenance again. It seems astonishing at first, even impossible, that such a petition should be made by the Son, but the direction of the Psalm leads to this conclusion, and if we accept this, what a vision of His filial submission and humility is revealed! He prays that death may not keep His body: He is willing to undergo the ordeal but prays to be preserved from eternal death. He trusts in the Father's mercy (v. 5) and by faith affirms that 'My heart shall rejoice in Thy salvation'. 'Salvation' in the Psalms is mystically equivalent to 'resurrection' when the word is in a Messianic context. It is moving to note in this connection that He does not express His trust in God's *power* (to raise up), but 'I have trusted in Thy *mercy*!' The punishment for sin must be borne ere He receive the resurrection; hence it is in the guise of mortal man (solemn thought) that He must trust the Father for the remission of the sins for which He would die. As man's Substitute He must plead God's mercy. When we in our turn need thus to plead, we too can say 'I have trusted in Thy mercy', for by Jesus' obedient descent into death and by His resurrection, God's forgiveness and mercy are proven.

He speaks now with confidence. There is a spiritual progression in this psalm which affords the dramatic vividness of experience: the mournful pleading, the petition, the anguished appeal, the act of faith, the concluding major key of joy and confidence, suggesting that between the last two points an unrecorded communication was received from above, an assurance of God's pledged word. Thus reassured, the Petitioner is quietly confident that 'salvation' (resurrection) will be vouchsafed, and the dark shadow of sorrow and dereliction melts away. His spirit then rises in gratitude (v. 6) and joy —

> I will sing unto the Lord, because He hath dealt
> bountifully with me!

A striking wealth of meaning may be found in this last phrase. The thanksgiving is not only for the reassurance and comfort received. It is an accepting by faith of an act still in the future as though it had already materialized. In John 13:3 Jesus was able to assert: 'Now is the Son of Man glorified' — even before His Passion was accomplished. He *hath dealt* bountifully with me. He has conceded what I asked. He has given full and abundant answer. The 'salvation' would be not only for Jesus' own body but for all those who should believe on Him!

What ineffable conference this was between the Father and the Son! His rejoicing will be great for the Father's sake, for on receiving the preservation of His body for ever, as He had petitioned, the enemies of God will be defeated, and though at the moment 'mine enemy' may be 'exalted over me', in the end he shall not be able to say he has prevailed. Jesus is jealous for the honour of God's Name. Having trusted Himself to God's promise, He knows that the enemy's undoing is certain.

PSALM 14

This psalm opens with the words: The fool hath said in his heart, There is no God.

Jesus, whose mind dwelt continually with the Father, saw

the wickedness around Him as it were in double perspective, with the eyes of God as well as those of the Righteous Man. Fools! The word describes the divine view of men's behaviour. God looks 'down from heaven upon the children of men, to see if there were any that did understand and seek God'. But He sees as Jesus did, that they are 'corrupt . . , abominable . . , filthy . . ,' and in fact —

There is none that doeth good, no, not one. (v. 3).

Have all the workers of iniquity no knowledge? He asks. (v. 4).
When they 'eat up the people as they eat bread', do they not know that the Lord is a refuge to the poor? These cogitations seem to be more apt in Jesus' time than even David's. He ejaculates with longing:

O that the salvation of Israel were come out of Zion! (v. 7)

For David it was an expression of longing; for the Messiah a way of saying how He was 'straightened until it be accomplished'. (Luke 12:50). The speaker looks forward to the time when the Lord shall 'bring back the captivity of His people' (v. 7) as though Jesus were contemplating with eager longing the finish of His redemptive work, when 'Jacob shall rejoice and Israel be glad'.

PSALM 15.

Here is an echo of Psalm 1. It has often been preached on as a portrait of the Just One, and seems to confirm that Psalm as not merely a blessing on the man who is upright, but as a protrait of the Only Begotten. It is a moment of quiet meditation which might have been the Messiah's as He entered the synagogue or the Temple, or even during the serene calm of His lonely vigils on the hilltop or in the olive-grove. There is a peacefulness about it that suggests quiet rumination as the mind sums up the qualities of the ideal or pattern on God's mind when He made man.

Though vile men and evil doing are mentioned, the tone is muted and the emphasis is on the Man who walketh uprightly: worketh righteousness, and speaketh the truth in his heart — the three positives for the three negatives of Psalm 1. The three negatives of this psalm, which now follow, are not limned in such strong colours as in the first Psalm. They are offences not so much against God as against man's fellows, and portray by contrast the courtesy and integrity of the meditator — 'backbiteth not with his tongue, nor doeth evil to his neighbour, nor taketh up a reproach against his neighbour; in whose eyes a vile person is condemned, who honours his word though it be to his own hurt, and changeth not.'

This is God's model Man, whom He loves. The tone seems to be more one with the gentle beauty of Christ than the warrior spirit of David. His meditation reaches its conclusion with

> He that doeth these things is never moved.

In these words may be discerned the deep stillness of His spirit. The whole psalm is composed in a key of spiritual repose which dwells steadily on the main note of the soul's profound peace. In concluding this psalm returns to the tonic note like the first movement of a symphony and denotes here a strong undercurrent of assurance, thus casting into perspective the phases of pain and disappointment in the preceding psalms. They were but momentary ruffles on the surface, that did not affect the depths.

Thus far the portrait emerges of a Man who thinks in terms of God, but whose nervous system is thoroughly human. His soul is strong and consciously upright; flawless in God's sight. This, and His uninterrupted communion with the Father, give Him a strong underlying peace and serenity which enables Him to keep His equanimity and outer calm in face of all sorts of opposition and recrimination. However, His sensitiveness is such that inwardly He often shrinks from the repeated contact with the sinfulness He observes around Him, and He is frequently roused to indignation by their perversity, especially that of the men who were teachers of God's holy Law to the people. The wish to avoid such company is coupled with a consciousness of His mission. The effect of His human sensitivity on His divine nature causes moral anguish which at times breaks out in tears when in private or bursts from Him in righteous anger, nay, Godlike wrath, during which, like Jehovah, He vows their destruction without mercy because they continue on their wicked way despite God's warnings. But He never loses sight of the day when, the government upon His shoulders (I Chron. 16:33) He shall judge in righteousness and shall administer justice in uprightness so that oppression shall be no more.

This was the joy that was set before Him: the pleasing of the Father through the accomplishment of man's rescue from the grip of Satan and the eventual imposition of universal rectitude in the dispensing of judgment. Despite the anguish and tears, despite moments of human weariness and disappointment, a holy joy habitually suffused His face, and though the features may have been settled in gravity, the light of ultimate victory shone with assurance through His eyes, illuming the sadness, like dew on the mown grass caught in the light of dawn.

PSALM 16.

As Jesus' missionary work continued, it became increasingly evident to Him that the wrath of the Pharisees and doctors of the Law would not be appeased but by His death. Their minds were already actively seeking means of doing away with Him. He did not keep their traditions and in their opinion He incited the people against them by His teachings. They angrily sought how to rid themselves of Him. Jesus knew this but with quiet courage He continued to give fearless and straight answers when they challenged Him to explain His behaviour. 'Why walk not Thy disciples according to the tradition of the elders?' they demanded. And Jesus looked straight at them as He answered: 'Well hath Esaias prophesied of you hypocrites,

This people honoureth me with their lips but their heart is far from me. Howbeit in vain they worship me, teaching for doctrine the commandments of men', and He adds: 'Full well ye reject the commandment of God, that ye may keep your own tradition . . . making the word of God of none effect through your tradition.' (Mark 7:6).

He was speaking from His own observation, but no doubt He would recall the words of God given through Jeremiah, that the priests laid burdens on these people 'which I commanded not, nor spake it, neither came it into my heart.'

Not content with defying those who had set themselves up as spiritual taskmasters over the people, He called to the bystanders and publicly refuted some of their pet traditions. The argument was so simple and the illustration so telling that they could not help but agree with Him, and by doing so, flout the authority of the elders. 'Hearken unto me, every one of you, and understand', He proclaimed, 'there is nothing from without a man that entering into him can defile him, because it entereth not into his heart, but into the belly and goeth out in the draught. But from within, out of the heart of man, proceed evil thoughts, covetousness, wickedness, deceit, lasciviousness, adultery, murder, pride, foolishness. These defile a man.' The 'elders' knew He had portrayed them. (Mark 7:20,23).

His words had the stamp of common sense and reality; their authority was undeniable, and His detractors gnashed their teeth in impotent rage. They were losing their stranglehold on the people. Their dominion would vanish unless they speeded up measures to eliminate this rebel.

Jesus knew their thoughts and realized that His time was short. No anger at their machinations against Him arose in His heart as it did when He beheld their offences against God. He knew His life must be forfeit and He was ready to make the sacrifice, fully conscious that for this purpose He had come into the world. He started to prepare His disciples for the inevitable. He began to teach them that the 'Son of man must suffer many things and be rejected of the elders, and of the chief priests, and scribes, and be killed; but He always reminded them of the other step beyond the apparently final one, the step that His enemies could not foresee but that He wished His disciples to know, that they might bear the sorrow that was coming upon them. So He added: '— and after three days rise again.'

His thoughts were serene at this time. He saw not the angry faces nor did He have qualms about the coming torture. His mind dwelt on the glory beyond the present, when they on earth would have done with Him. At His baptism the 'heavens were opened unto Him', and they probably remained so though men did not see this. More, we may deduce from this (16th) Psalm that His spirit longed for the peace of His heavenly abode, for the eyes of His soul looked past death, to the Father's right hand:

> In Thy presence is fulness of joy:
> At Thy right hand are pleasures of ever more. (v. 1).

This truth was not a vision in a moment of rapture, nor an escapist's dream under disillusion and misery. It was the goal of His thoughts, a permanent reality that He strove towards; it was what gave Him His calm courage, His perseverance, and His steady endurance.

Through the prophetic inspiration of this Davidic psalm we know how He addressed His soul to the combat:

> O my soul, thou hast said unto the Lord, Thou art my
> Lord: my goodness extendeth not to thee.
> But to the saints that are in the earth, and to the
> excellent in whom is all my delight.

What other meaning can that strange clause have — 'My goodness extendeth not to thee' — but that it is the dual nature of our Lord communing with the Father? God's reply to His avowal 'Thou art my Lord' is that His goodness shall henceforth embrace not only His Son who is righteous, but overflow to the 'saints that are in the earth'. Perhaps we may clarify the meaning as: My goodness extendeth not to thee alone.

The mission of Jesus was already accomplishing something: it was turning some men's hearts back to God, and by healing the diseased He was pointing the way to those who had fallen under God's wrath. One recalls the words of

Deborah's song: O my soul, thou hast trodden down strength! Enemy territory was already being invaded.

The second part of the psalm is on a different subject.

Was He saddened sometimes by the thought of having to leave the beauty of the earth so soon? Did He ever regret the fact that His was but a short stay, that it was not for Him as yet to enjoy in possession? The thought seems to have brought a touch of sadness for something He had come to love, for there is resoluteness in:

The Lord is the portion of mine inheritance and of my cup:
Thou maintainest my lot.

As He looked about Him around Galilee, at the heliotrope hills and the violet lake, at the trees and the vineyards, at the wild flowers and the children, His heart loved them and He surely enjoyed being there among them. This was His land, this the portion of the earth that God had chosen as the place to set His name, and His own feet were treading its surface.

The lines are fallen unto me in pleasant places,
Yea, I have a goodly heritage.—

Thus perhaps He would muse as He observed the countryside of northern Palestine. Over this nation would His throne eventually be raised; this land which God had given to Abraham was His own, for He was of Abraham's seed, and of Judah's. He was the King of Israel.

But His heritage was more than this land and this people. It included also the millions in other climes and future ages who would believe on His name and be saved. Meanwhile He could face the ordeal of angry accusations and rise easily above the capcious questions. He knew their posers before they brought them, versed as He was in the Scriptures, understanding them in a light to which the Pharisees were blind. It was God who counselled Him, and during His nightly vigils of prayer and communion on the hillside He received His instructions:

I will bless the Lord who hath given me counsel:
My reins also instruct me in the night seasons. (v. 7).

68

Perhaps here we may dimly see answered the question of whether He was divinely omniscient while on earth in the flesh. It may well be that He depended for guidance on His heavenly Father, as men do who know God, but unlike men, His contact with God remained always unbroken.

I have set the Lord always before me:
Because He is at my right hand, I shall not be moved.

Jesus could feel His Father constantly with Him as He moved forward to what in men's eyes was His doom. Thus He could say — 'I shall not be moved' — either from His purpose or by the dread of what He was called to undergo, and He could face with serenity, even with gladness, the worst that men could do to Him —

Therefore my heart is glad and my glory rejoiceth:
My flesh also shall rest in hope.

'. . . — and rise again', He told His disciples, not once but many times. They did not understand, thinking He referred to the final resurrection of all men, but Jesus contemplated a reality that was immediate and literal:

For Thou wilt not leave my soul in hell:
Neither wilt Thou suffer Thine Holy One to see corruption.

And again —

Thou wilt show me the path of life;
In Thy presence is fullness of joy,
And at Thy right hand are pleasures for ever more.

Not the suffering but the sweetness of hope and the joy of the Father's presence was what occupied His mind as He entered the last year of His sojourn on earth; for, as for His flesh, it would rise again, and for ever more He was to keep the bodily form He had assumed for the redemption of men.

☆ ☆ ☆

PSALM 17.

The cry of this psalm comes from a soul locked in mortal combat with an enemy having power to deal mortal blows. Dare we contemplate the picture that arises as we place the words in the experience of Christ?

By doing so, it becomes evident that Jesus was not sublimely indifferent to the attacks of the Evil One. He could not continue on His way as though Satan did not exist. Daily, hourly, there was a hand-to-hand struggle as the Enemy battled for supremacy. Through the hatred inspired in the Jewish leaders, the devil continually sought to destroy Jesus (John 8:44), or by any means to prevent the consummation of His mission.

From this Psalm (continuing in our assumption that David's psalms disclose episodes in Jesus' inner experience), it would appear that the powers of darkness gave Him no respite. Much that was never recorded in the Gospels for the simple reason that Jesus would not and could not speak of these battles to mortal man, was prophetically spoken by David who wrote these words unconscious, perhaps, of their full import. This is a vigorous account of unremitting spiritual warfare. The dramatic fact emerges that for Jesus it was a very real battle, the outcome of which hung on His spirit's strength and to some extent on His physical endurance. In the previous Psalm He cried, 'Preserve me, O God'. Now He appeals to God to

> Hear the right, O Lord, attend unto my cry,
> Give ear unto my prayer.

These are words of a soul in hard-pressed wrestling. The tone is urgent, the repeated clauses suggest an agony of supplication. Did He wonder sometimes if His flesh could hold out until the Sacrifice was made and God's will accomplished? On earth, where Satan's dominion had been established, Jesus was exposed to all the weaponry that the enemy could muster. It cannot have been easy for Him. Here, behind the scene, is presented a picture of Christ very different from that of the outwardly meek and lowly Jesus. Here is the Happy Warrior for Whom victory does not come easily in a struggle being fought every inch of the way. It was a mortal struggle as Satan exerted every wile to prevent the act of Redemption and to snatch victory from the Being whom he held to be rival for the dominion and the allegiance of men. A wrestling, almost sinewy effect is produced in the words by means of the short vigorous sentences, almost like laboured breathing through clenched teeth —

> Let my sentence come forth from Thy presence:
> Let Thine eyes behold the things that are equal.
> Thou hast proved mine heart; Thou hast visited
>   me in the night;
> Thou has tried me, and shalt find nothing.

Surely only the Son of God could truthfully claim this. That His struggle was with the Evil One is evident from verses 12,13. His enemy crouches like a lion greedy of its prey, and He calls on the Lord to . . .

> Arise and disappoint him, cast him down,
>   and deliver my soul.

One may ask if the last clause of v. 3 is to be included in the possible thoughts of Jesus in this warfare? Could He have said:

> I am purposed that my mouth shall not transgress —?

It may be so. It is certainly an integral part of the prayer. If we think that His virile spirit must often have realized how at a word He could wipe out the 'deadly enemies' who compassed Him about (v. 9). Yet He had to withhold His righteous wrath and continue meekly on the way which led to Calvary. It is possible that Jesus had to exercise a conscious restraint at times to prevent His godly indignation from breaking out and speaking the word that would have felled them.

The fourth verse would suggest that Jesus had to depend very closely on the Father whose Envoy He was, to carry out the plan of Salvation to the letter — 'Concerning the works of men, by the word of Thy lips have I kept me from the path of the destroyer. Hold up my goings in Thy paths, that my footsteps slip not.' We know that He could not sin, but He too had to beware of the enemy's snares and to be constantly on His guard lest He be deflected from His path. His footsteps could not 'slip' in the sense of sinning, but He had to seek the will of the Father for every step. The many journeys He made were not haphazard. Every one was a 'going in Thy paths'.

His prayer continues —

I have called upon Thee, for Thou wilt hear me, O God.

In His prayer at the tomb of Lazarus He could say, I thank Thee that Thou hearest me always. Because of the people that stood by He said it aloud then, but in His private intercessions He had proved it many a time before.

> Keep me as the apple of the eye,
> Hide me under the shadow of Thy wings.

Jesus could have prayed these words, for He knew how important it was that He should be kept. He would be familiar with the Song of Moses who says that God kept him as the apple of His eye. (Deut. 32:10) and with Zachariah's words (2:8), 'He that toucheth you toucheth the apple of his eye . . . and ye shall know that the Lord of host hath sent me.' Jesus trusts the Father for the care of His person, the most precious human form ever to be born, most precious of all because it had to reach the altar of sacrifice undamaged. And finally on the Cross He committed His spirit to God's keeping as He made ready to breach the defences of Hell, there to challenge His arch-enemy face to face on his own territory in the very realms of death.

Finally this psalm considers how the 'men of the world' are 'full of children and leave the rest of their substance to their babes'. It appears to be a punishment on the ungodly that they die before their children are grown. In the children He brought to the Father Jesus will see of the travail of His soul. 'As for me', the psalmist concludes,

> I will behold Thy face in righteousness;
> I shall be satisfied when I awake with Thy likeness.

Jesus was One with the Father, the 'image of the Father' (II Cor. 4:4; Col. 1:15). His children will have His likeness stamped upon them (Rom. 8:29) for they will be 'conformed to His image'. On entering into the life everlasting that His steadfastness had won for them, they (and we among them) too will be fully satisfied on awakening with *His* likeness!

☆   ☆   ☆

PSALM 18.

In warrior terms David praises God, giving thanks for a deliverance:

> I will love Thee; O Lord, my strength;
> The Lord is my rock, my fortress and my deliverer . . .
> My buckler, and the horn of my salvation, and my
>   high tower.
> I will call upon the name of the Lord who is
>   worthy to be praised
> So shall I be saved from mine enemies.

Then the situation from which he had been delivered is described:

> The sorrows of hell compassed me about;
> The snares of death prevented me.
> In my distress I called upon the Lord. (vs. 5,6).

The divine intervention is described in the imagery of a great storm with thunder and lightening, black clouds so heavy that the heavens are 'bowed down'; flailing hailstones like coals of fire (v. 7-16) are flung to the ground, reverberating thunderbolts strike the earth so that it shakes and trembles, and a mighty wind, 'the blast of the breath of Thy nostrils' uncovers the foundations of the deep.

David speaks of an escape from death (v. 4,5) of having 'run through a troop', and 'leaped over a wall' (v. 29), so he appears to have eluded the enemy, for God had made his feet 'like hinds' feet' (v. 33), It is not till later in the psalm that he speaks in quite different terms of battle and final victory. (vs. 34-42,48).

If we seek a parallel in Jesus' experience, such an occasion of deliverance from the clutches of His enemies can be found quite early in His public life. He had been preaching in the synagogue. They rose up and thrust Him out of the city and led Him 'unto the brow of the hill ... that they might cast Him headlong. But He *passing through the midst* of them, went His way (Luke 4:22-30).

On other occasions when men took up stones to kill Him (John 10:31-39) His life was humanly speaking endangered, for He had said, 'I and my Father are one', and 'Before Abraham was, I AM', which in the ears of the Jews was blasphemy and worthy of death by stoning. The threat was of severe physical injury, almost certain death, and perhaps a real thuderstorm suddenly breaking over their heads at that moment as described in the psalm enabled Him to elude their fierce intent. God thundered in the heavens and the Highest gave His voice. He shot out lightenings and discomfited them. The words of the psalm fit the circumstances so well that suddenly the scene becomes vividly real, while we actually learn what may have been His unspoken thoughts during the occasion. Jesus, escaping out of their hands, could say —

> He sent from above, He took me, He drew me
> out of many waters

— the waters of a senseless mob, satanically inspired, who would have destroyed Him —

> He delivered me from my strong enemy and
> from them which hated me.

The crisis over, He could say:

> He brought me forth also into a large place
> He delivered me because He delighted in me. (v. 19).

Confidently we may ascribe to Jesus these words, for the voice of God stated this publicly on more than one occasion. The Speaker in this psalm is at once identified as the Man described in the First Psalm, the master-pattern. He is the

Man whose delight is in the Law of the Lord and in His Law doth meditate day and night. None but the righteous Son of God could claim without self-deception that He had kept all the ways of the Lord and that He was upright before God. It is the Righteous Man of Psalm 1 and 15 who now says with simple candor:

> The Lord rewarded me according to my righteousness;
> According to the cleanness of my hands hath He
>   recompensed me.
> For I have kept the ways of the Lord and have not
>   departed from my God,
> For all His judgments were before me, and I did not
>   put away His statutes from me.

We find more of these thoughts in Psalm 119.

When the 'sorrows of death' did later engulf Him, He was 'brought forth into a large place', for God then raised Him up and gave Him the seat at His right hand, crowned with glory and honour. (I Pet. 1:21; Heb. 2:9) and His kingdom shall have no end.

When He answered the loaded questions of His enemies or was faced with their open accusations, He did so always with the calm assurance of the Man who knows His God and is familiar with His Law. He openly discomfited them so easily that after a time they durst not ask Him any more questions. (Mat. 22:46) Hence He could have said in the words of this Psalm (v. 37) —

> I have pursued mine enemies and have overtaken them,
> Neither did I turn again until they were consumed.
> I have wounded them that they were not able to rise . . .

— 'The baptism of John, was it from heaven, or of men? And they reasoned with themselves, saying, If we shall say, From heaven, he will say, Why then did ye not believe him? But it we say, Of men, they feared the people, for all men counted John that he was prophet indeed. And they answered and said to Jesus, We cannot tell. And Jesus answered, Neither do I tell you by what authority I do these things.'

. . . They are fallen under my feet . . .
Thou hast delivered me from the strivings of the people.

They often marvelled at the swiftness and the simplicity of His arguments, so simple that they were unanswerable. 'Whose is the superscription?' It made them look so foolish. Then He stood in the temple and said aloud to all the crowd that had gathered round, 'Beware of the scribes, which love to go in long clothing and love respectful salutations in the market and the chief seats in the synagogue and devour widows' houses and for a pretence make long prayers: these shall receive greater damnation' — And the common people heard Him gladly.

Thou hast delivered me from the strivings of the people and Thou hast made me the head of the heathen: (v. 43).

It was just after His escape (Luke 4) that men began to acknowledge His authority and power and 'His fame went out into every place of the country round about' (Luke 4:36,37). Again, when He openly avowed that He was the Son of God (John 10:31-33) and was doing the work for which His Father had sent Him, and was about to be stoned, 'He went away beyond Jordan into the place where John first baptized, and there He abode. And many resorted unto Him and said, John did no miracle, but all things that John spoke of this man were true. And many believed on Him there. (John 10:36-42). A 'large place'!

As soon as they hear me, they shall obey me:
The strangers shall submit themselves unto me. (v. 44).

He went away beyond Jordan and it was there that the 'strangers' and the 'heathen' believed in Him. The psalm tells the same story, (v. 43): 'Thou hast made me the head of the heathen' — (not as in v. 40, 'given me the necks of' — which applies to 'mine enemies', but 'made me the head of the heathen'!).

The psalm concludes with thanks and praise 'unto thee, O Lord, among the heathen', where He will 'sing praises unto Thy name'. Surely these might have been his words as

He abode there beyond Jordan, remembering the promise, 'I will give thee the heathen for thine inheritance'. The closing words were written for Him by His ancestor, David —

> Great deliverance giveth He to His King;
> And showeth mercy to His anointed,
> To David and to his seed for ever.

PSALM 19.

'The heavens declare the glory of God'. It has been claimed that the first part of this psalm is from an ancient hymn to the sun by a heathen author and incorporated into his poem by the Hebrew psalmist! It is a conclusive argument against this suggestion that again it is the Righteous Man of Psalm 1 speaking in praise of the holiness of God's law. If we think of the first half of the psalm as the prelude to a hymn on the beauty and perfection of God's Law, and lay stress on the verb 'declare', proclaim, the true meaning of the poetic introduction becomes apparent.

The Son, in co-existence with the Father, had been present at the Creation of the universe when its laws were laid down. There is something in the regularity and precision of all the movements of the heavenly bodies that uniquely speaks of the mind of God. The laws of nature have never been affected or altered, nor can they be until the great and terrible day of the Lord shall come. Myriads of shining spheres revolve in their orbits unchanging, their mathematical exactitude having about it something of the sublimity of the Mind that fashioned them. When Jesus would walk out to Bethany or Bethsaida, Samaria or Capernaum, he would see the heavens from man's viewpoint and so, with new eyes. And since His mind was continually occupied with the Law of the Lord, meditating on it day and night, He may well have exclaimed on looking up at the firmament how eloquently God's glory is declared in His handiwork. How could men fail to see this? There it was, so obviously patterned by the same Will that made the Law: perfect, sure, wise and right. It *declared* the glory of God.

How often Jesus was saddened and surprised that men could not understand. He had often asked the question, even of His disciples, 'Do not ye yet understand?' He had taught them by preaching, He had demonstrated by miracles, He had explained by analogies, and yet to the very last they had failed to grasp His real mission. The Pharisees had quite lost sight of the sublimity of God in their fanatical slavery to their own petty traditions. Their minds were mean and low. 'How is it that ye do not understand?' He would ask in pain and wonderment. And then walking along the country road He would see the glorious sun in its majestic journey across the sky. It would appear so obviously to be declaring God's glory! The very heavens are a witness! How can men say they need a sign! And from contemplation of the starred heavens at night and of the golden glory of the morning, His mind would return to its meditation in the Law. The second half of this psalm develops for us something of how 'in His law doth He meditate day and night'.

Here are some of His meditations on God's Law: He thinks of its perfection, its justice, its truth, its goodness, its preciousness, its purity, its reliability for guidance and warning.

Yes, to Him it was so plain that He may have wondered that men could not hear how

> Day after day uttereth speech and night after night
>   sheweth knowledge,
> There is no speech nor language where their voice
>   is not heard.

— so to the very farthest corners of the earth the same testimony was given.

No doubt certain petitions in the psalms cannot be ascribed to the thinking of Christ, and yet we may ponder them in that light. Here is a passage of this sort:

> Cleanse Thou me from secret faults.
> Keep back Thy servant from presumptuous sins . . .
> Then . . . I shall be innocent from the great
>   transgression. (vs. 12,13).

78

If we think of the Temptation here, it would have been 'presumtuous sin' to cast Himself down from the Temple height to prove that He was the Son of God, quite apart from the fact that it is unthinkable, since to have put God's Word to the test in this way would have been to obey an injunction of Satan. It was the devil's 'Hath God said', again. Obedience to the Tempter would have been '*the* great transgression' (v. 13), and He remained innocent of it. He had no 'faults' (v. 12) to be cleansed. But it is noteworthy that this word is in italics, as evidently absent from the original. If, as in some versions, it means 'needs', it is not unlawful to suppose that Jesus would pray that His human frame might be kept in subjection, its requirements restrained. He spoke firmly and frankly of this in private to His disciples. (Mat. 19:11,12).

The comparison in this psalm with the sun starting on its glorious journey like a bridegroom coming out of his chamber and 'rejoicing as a strong man to run a race', is a beautiful one. So the Sun of Righteousness arose, and after His public presentation girded Himself in the wilderness as a strong man to run the race that was set before Him, His body being the 'tabernacle' for the divine Second Person, whose 'going forth is from the end of heaven and His circuit unto the ends of it' — completing His circuit with His return to the Father!

PSALM 20.

Because of the vocabulary of warfare in verses 5 and 7, 'set up our banners', 'chariots and horses', the prayer that 'The Lord hear thee . . ., defend thee, sent thee help from the sanctuary, strengthen thee, remember all thy offerings, grant . . ., fulfill . . .' (vs. 1-4) suggests these words as apt for the priestly benediction of an army on the eve of battle. The variety of the pronouns in the rest of the psalm suggests that other voices make response — 'thee' in verses 1-4; 'we' in vs. 5,8; 'I', v. 6; 'they', v. 8. Thus it would appear that vs. 1-4 are the priest's blessing, vs. 5,7,8 the people's answer (we). Who then is the 'I' of v. 6? Was it the priest or the warrior himself, or a third party? And who says in v. 9, 'Save, Lord, let the King hear', etc? The dialogue structure is interesting.

An occasion in the life of our Lord to which this psalm may apply will be found by seeking for someone who might have uttered these blessings on Jesus. The blessing is a lovely one. It would be appropriate to think of — '. . . the Lord strengthen thee . . . accept thy sacrifice . . . grant thee thy heart's desire; . . . fulfill all thy petition' — as spoken by John the Baptist as Jesus rose out of the water. John was a Levite and would have the authority to bless in the name of the Lord God of Jacob. This would be particularly apt at the beginning of Jesus' public ministry and the purpose for which He came.

But there is a deeper and richer hidden application, combining all these elements in the psalm: blessing, warrior imagery, and variety of pronouns. At the Baptism the father's Voice spoke out and the Spirit descended upon the Son, bringing the Trinity together at that significant moment. We may therefore think of this psalm as the Holy Spirit's blessing on the Son at the start of His mission. From this point of view there is no difficulty in identifying the "I" of v. 6.

In the change from singular to plural in v. 5 —

> We will rejoice in thy salvation,
> and in the name of the Lord we will set up
> our banners —

we seem to hear the heavenly chorus joining in as the angels and holy ones all speed Him on His way, and add their prayer:

> The Lord fulfil all thy petitions.

The pronoun 'I' enters in v. 6, as though it were the response from Jesus' own heart —

> Now know I that the Lord saveth His anointed;
> He will hear from His holy heaven with the strength
> of His right hand.

With this saving strength to uphold Him He would be able to face the scoffers, the tempters, the critics and the betrayer; all His enemies would be 'brought down and fallen' (v. 8), but He would rise and 'stand upright', His righteousness proven and His claims confirmed by His resurrection. He could go steadily up to Jerusalem with the confidence that God would hear Him from His holy heaven with the saving strength of His right hand. Though His eyes contemplated the coming battle He could rest in the assurance that His trust in God would be vindicated. This confidence adds even greater poignancy to the agonized cry from the Cross of: My God, why hast *Thou* forsaken me?

The blessings of this psalm are equally apt for the close of the Messiah's public life and could have been words of divine comfort received as the angels 'ministered unto Him' in Gethsemane as Jesus addressed Himself to the final battle, for Psalm 20 is the starting point of a sequence that builds up from a point before and passes through the period of the Crucifixion with its faith, agony and hope, to the triumphal entry into heaven of the Victory, with Psalm 24.

PSALM 21.

In the reports of Jesus' words written in the Gospels it is evident that His goal was constantly in His thoughts. The Messiah in the Psalms also habitually contemplates the glorious future kingdom. The more threatening the surroundings, the brighter shone the vision. Thus it was 'for the JOY that was set before Him He endured the cross'. The sequence here of Psalm 21 with its joyful thanksgiving for the victory coming after the cry for succour ending Psalm 20, follows the same pattern, for the thanks are offered *before* the victory is materially won, for the crux comes in the next psalm. The future event is taken by faith as factual, such as when in Jesus' intercessory prayer before Gethsemane, He could say, I have finished the work that Thou gavest me to do, though the Cross lay still ahead. There is a hint of the timelessness of the divine Mind in this. At the very scene of His rejection Jesus could refer to His coming in the glory of the Father with the holy angels (Luke 22:69). So here He confidently proclaims that

> The king shall joy in Thy strength, O Lord,
> And in Thy salvation how greatly shall he rejoice!

The tense is still future, as in Psalm 13:5,6).

The words, 'Thou hast given him his heart's desire' (v. 2) might well have expressed the grateful prayer of Jesus on more than one occasion. In His intercessory prayer of John 17 He asks one special favour — the only time He expressed His own will to the Father — 'Father, I will that they whom Thou hast given to me, be with me where I am'. A few hours before, He had stated as a fact: 'I go to prepare a place for you, that where I am, there ye may be also.' Thus in this psalm, He speaks of having already received what He petitions:

> Thou hast given him his heart's desire,
> And hast not withholden the request of his lips.

The 'Selah' that follows would be pregnant with meaning for Him.

We are told (v. 4) what His request had been:

> He asked life of thee and thou gavest it him,
> Even length of days, for ever and ever.

Jesus Himself says (John 5:26) 'As the Father hath life in Himself, so hath He given to the Son to have life in Himself.' As He went over this Psalm He would also think of the prophecy in Isaiah 53:10, 'When Thou shalt make His soul an offering for sin, He shall see His seed, He shall prolong His days, . . . He shall see of the travail of His soul and be satisfied. 'He asked . . . Thou gavest'; 'His heart's desire . . .' . . . 'satisfied'!

In the Psalmist's words we get a glimpse of the vista which the eyes of Jesus inwardly contemplated: the abundant life which through His sacrifice would be available to man, life which would be 'length of days for ever and ever'.

The eternal life which He enjoyed would be shared with all who accepted His mediation.

The crown of pure gold (v. 3), the honour and majesty with which God has clothed Him are His. If the faithful servant shall receive the glorious commendation, 'Well done . . . enter thou into the joy of thy Lord,' how much more so would the faithful Son receive the reward of His work! He was made 'exceeding glad' (v. 6) by the approving countenance of the Father when He was received back into glory, having opened the way for the children whom God would give Him.

As a contrast His wicked enemies will have the frown of God's anger. And their seed will be 'cut off'. The reason given, 'For they intended evil against Thee'. It was not only Jesus whom they rejected; it was the Father, and by faith in His coming victory He could say, (v. 11):

> They imagined a mischievous device which they
> were not able to perform.

Men crucified and buried Him but they did not put an end to Him, for He rose again.

It is not out of place to think of our Lord Jesus joining in the song of praise to the Father when He and the redeemed shall be together in glory: So shall we sing and praise Thy power. (v. 13). His thoughts were constantly upon the joy He spoke of in John 15:11 — 'that my joy may remain in you, and that your joy might be full'.

However, the point we are seeking is not how far these psalms express the thoughts of Christ but rather what kind of mind is at work here and what portrait emerges as a result of examining that mind. It is evident that much that is enclosed in such psalms as this is not limited to the experience of David; more, some statements would appear presumptuous if spoken by sinful man. It is true that the heart that is cleansed may enjoy re-established communion with God, and many a pardoned sinner has found in these psalms exquisitely expressed his own sad experience. But these heights and depths of spiritual feeling, sensitiveness and communion exceed human proportions even when we take into account that David was not only a tough warrior but the sweet singer. David was in more ways than one the man after God's own heart.

This twenty-first Psalm has been called a 'Coronation Psalm' and may have been written by David for his ceremonial coronation, or about it afterwards; and it may well have been sung as a coronation hymn for the more godly kings of Judah who succeeded him. Yet there is no doubt that phrases like 'He asked of Thee . . . length of days for ever and ever' (v. 4), have reverberations that transcend the occasion and belong to the future Messiah. As David's psalms — conscious or unconsciously — project into the thoughts and inner experiences of Christ, they cease to be hyperboles and become sublime statements of fact. And if the phrase, 'For Thou hast made him most blest for ever' (v. 6), be thought of as pertaining to Christ, what follows should not be rejected as His also; rather, the new angles from which the rest of the psalm may be viewed should be examined. The terrible lines which devout readers sometimes deplore as 'unchristian vindictiveness', such as v. 9 —

> Thou shalt make them (that hate Thee) as a fiery
> oven in the time of Thine anger —

will be seen not as angry inprecations but a solemn statement of truth. Jesus knew what fate awaits wicked men in the purposes of God.

> The Lord shall swallow them up in His Wrath
> and the fire shall devour them.

It was in view of precisely that fact that God sent His Son to their rescue, and the Son willingly came. This is not vengeful thinking, but fact. Words like 'Thou hast made Him most blessed for ever' are the hallmark of the Speaker, and by it all the rest must be gauged.

—What, then, are the features of the portrait that we find emerging? From Psalm 16 to the present one, Psalm 21, we see a mind of quite unusual fortitude, uprightness, firmness and courage, coupled with a heart of more than human sensitiveness and sweetness; a strange amalgam of humility and boldness, fear and trust, anguish and sublime confidence; a man going through a severe testing yet enabled to do so with equanimity because spiritually he beholds the face of God in righteousness and he is able to enjoy in anticipation limitless joy that will be his when the trial is over. Though He knows deep anguish and great joy, His characteristic is the quiet serenity of confidence. His is a mind stayed upon God, sustained by meditation in His Law; it is a soul that worships, acknowledging the supremacy of God; (Jesus said, 'The Father is greater than I') — yet its natural language is co-equal with God's. A strong soul, it must however seek strength in God for the task assigned to it; though expressing firm determination it is not self-confident, but constantly waits on God for sustenance and for deliverance from those who seek to destroy Him. It is a human heart of love and devotion and rare sweetness, but urged on by a divine view of the consequences of sin. Tenderness and sternness are blended.

Are not these qualities ratified as a portrait of Jesus Himself by that given of Him in the Gospels? We can, in fact, claim that these psalms provide a recognizable picture of Christ and fill in with colour the outline given by the Evangelists.

☆   ☆   ☆

PSALM 22.

Considering the habitual confidence, serenity and quiet joy evinced by the Righteous Man in the Psalms, the cry that opens the 22nd is quite startling in its agony. Even read in isolation from its context, the cry, 'My God, my God, why hast Thou forsaken me?' is the most desolate ever to come from human lips. Its sound echoes down the centuries and about the spheres until the whole universe reverberates hollowly and void of comfort. Much is involved in that cry as wrung from the heart of Jesus, the Immortal Son of God. We know that these words were pronounced by Him on the Cross. Whether He was quoting, or whether He recited this psalm to Himself, speaking only the first verse aloud, or whether the cry was wrung from Him, as we believe, when the guilt of the world was laid upon Him, (thus showing the Psalm to be prophetic), we cannot tell; but such a setting suggests that it was not just an apt quotation. It was a real and heart-rent cry that burst from Him in sudden anguish. The sharpness with which such an exclamation was forced from Him testifies not only to the stark reality of the helplessness and terror of humanity without God which Jesus then shared, but also, coming as it does in the silence of the opening, it conveys the startled surprise of a mortal wound received unexpectedly from a trusted hand falling upon a heart made vulnerable by confidence. Pain is mingled with horror and astonishment at the double blow.

Is this significance to be read into the experience of the Saviour? The crucifixion was not unexpected, for He had alluded to it; death was not a surprise, for He had foretold it; suffering caught Him not unawares for He had accepted the Cup. All had been borne silently and patiently in the knowledge and acceptance that this was part of the divine assignment. Then suddenly out of the silence burst this ringing agony. One asks in deepest awe, Was the dereliction unforeseen? Certain information was kept from the Son, as Jesus on occasion said, '. . . of that day and that hour knoweth no man, no . . . neither the Son, but the Father (only). Mark 13:32. Fore-knowledge of the dereliction to come when He was about to die, could in pity have been withheld from the loving heart of the Son until the time came. Jesus experienced the frightful darkness of the burden of sin that robbed Him of the felt Presence of His God.

His life was sinless. He had most zealously guarded His lips and thoughts from transgressing the Father's will. His care had been to keep Himself unspotted, in the world but not of it, to offer Himself wholly and undefiled to God as a ransom. Always He had enjoyed uninterrupted communion with His Father, and during His life on earth there had come never a shadow between. Now He is cut off.

The Righteous Man has always counted on divine help

and had taken for granted His intercourse with God. It was the natural consequence of His righteouness from the beginning, but at the supreme moment this was denied Him. Bound to the Cross by His love and His obedience, He found Himself open to the Powers of Evil, and, as men's sins were laid upon His shuddering soul, He discovered with greatest horror that He was alone. At this fearful crux He cries out: My God, my God, why hast *THOU* forsaken Me?

Seen away from the familiar narrative of the Crucifixion and placed in a context of calm assurance and praise (between Psalms 21 and 23), the cry comes the more startlingly. Trusting to the mighty arm of God, the Righteous Man had faced death, and that willingly, as the sacrifice of Himself for the sins of the world. John tells us, 'Jesus, knowing all things that should come upon Him, went forth . . .', and then states what things, the physical indignities and the manner of the sacrifice; but as we contemplate with mingled sorrow and terror the effect obtained by the initial position of this anguished exclamation, the realization comes of how the aversion of the Father's face wounded Christ. It reveals, surely, that though Jesus was the Son of God, and 'endured the Cross despising the shame', He did so not as a stoic tensed to insensitivity, or by sublimating Himself above it. The rod of God's wrath *struck* Him with a shocking jolt. The starkness with which the '*WHY?*' breaks out implies that He cannot have foreseen that communion with the Father would be cut off. The dereliction levelled a shaft at filial love and trust more awful than the worst He had expected. His identification with the lost was total.

After the first terrible outburst, the psalm continues mainly on the plane of physical suffering, though with spiritual agitation. The Sufferer had been subjected morally and physically to the most abject humiliation. He argues that God heard and delivered men that trusted in Him of old, why not now? And why not the speaker? He has reached the nadir of human experience: 'I am a worm and no man; a reproach of men and despised of the people.' this expresses not merely a sense of physical degradation but also the spiritual condition of man without God.

Further projection into the scene of Calvary follows:

All they that see me laugh me to scorn;
They shoot out the lip, they shake their heads, saying,
He trusted on the Lord that He would deliver him:
Let him deliver him, seeing He delighted in him. (v. 8).

Jesus, the Heir to the house of David, of the royal line of
Judah, must have borne Himself with natural majesty. At
times even His silence had been so regal and commanding
that His enemies had withdrawn in confusion. But now he
must submit to the scoffing, the jeers and the scorn, —He,
who had foretold that His detractors would see Him one
day sitting at the right hand of Power.

As he hung on the cross, surrounded by the rough mob
mocking Him in triumph, they must have appeared just as
v. 13 describes them:

They gaped at me with their mouths,
as ravening and roaring lions . . .
Wild dogs have encompassed me.

He was not beyond the hurt of their malevolence. The
tone here would suggest that He felt deeply their virulent
hate, and even the indifference of the executioners did not
go unregarded — as the present tense shows:

They part my garments among them,
and cast lots upon my vesture.

This picture, witnessed personally from His position on
the Cross, is poignant in the extreme. Hoisted up where He
was he could see the men actually sharing His raiment
among themselves as perquisites, and avidly casting lots for
His seamless vesture. Then, stripped as He now was, and
by His fixed posture compelled to look down, He could 'see
all (His) bones'. They seemed to stare back at Him, 'out of
joint', probably dislocated, distorting the harmonious beauty
of His perfect physique. No spiritual balm eased His
torment and not even a garment cloaked Him from the
harsh mockery of men. Like Adam with sin upon him, He

knew that he was naked.

There follows the catalogue of His less visible torture:

I am poured out like water, . . . my heart is like wax; . . .
My strength is dried up like potsherd,
And my tongue cleaveth to my jaws.
They pierced my hands and my feet . . .

Weakness was alien to the Man like a tree planted by rivers of water; now His heart is like wax. The burden of sin made Him feel human frailty in a way that he had never before experienced. 'Forasmuch then as the children are partakers of flesh and blood, He also Himself likewise took part of the same . . . For verily He took not on Him the nature of angels, but . . . the seed of Abraham. Therefore in all things it behoved him to be made like unto his bretheren, to make reconciliation for the sins of the people. (Heb. 2:14-17).

The 22nd Psalm is perhaps the most significantly Messianic of all the psalms. It is generally accepted as voicing thoughts of Jesus at a certain hour in His earthly life. As these psalms are studied side by side with the narrative of events in the Gospels the parallel becomes more and more evident, lending to the conviction that in all David's psalms divine inspiration led to the duality of identity. David wrote of pain and anguish of a kind that was outside his personal experience. What did David know of crucifixion, for instance? Absolutely nothing. It was unheard of, and yet his description of its particular type of suffering is vivid. David could not have undergone this himself. Perhaps he did not know the full import of his words. But ascribed to their true Author, the foreshadowed Messiah, the psalms together portray Someone other than the man who wrote them. The portrait that emerges is undeniably the Messiah's.

David's words transcend the actual and express feelings and thought sublimely greater than would have been comprehended in his own sphere. Inspiration lifted him onto a different plane of experience.

As he 'entered into the cloud' as it were, his soul would be 'cast down and disquieted within' him, feeling upon itself the indefinable burden of the Suffering Servant. The moral and physical agony here depicted so vividly in the first person seems actually to have been endured by the writer impersonating the Messiah.

How movingly lovely is the modulation to the major key coming at v. 22; After the torment of 'Be not far from me, O Lord . . . Deliver me . . . Save me . . .' and the imagery of the 'power of the dog', 'the mouth of the lion', the 'horns of the unicorns', comes the clear sweetness of

I will declare Thy name unto my brethren.

It marks the spirit's return to its habitual equanimity as soon as God's wrath is over and His vicarious sacrifice is accepted.

'My brethren'. The term gives a beautiful insight into His feeling for those whose experience He has now shared, and extends beyond those who had been Jesus' companions on earth to include all those who should be redeemed by His death. 'Who are my brethren?' He had asked when requested to return to the family home at Nazareth, and Himself had replied: My brethren are those that do the will of God. He had fulfilled that will, being made subject to death. He can declare the name of Jehovah the Saviour to those who are now His brethren. 'Go tell my brethren', He bid the women on the Resurrection morn, 'that I ascend unto my Father and *your Father* —'. He had won for them that privileged relationship and in a very real way He is now 'the Firstborn among many brethren'. (Rom. 8:28), whom God shall conform to the image of His Son.

In Isaiah's prophetic description of the Messiah's saviour-hood, we find the same beautiful change of key (63:1-9) —

I have trodden the winepress alone; . . . I looked
     and there was none to help; and I wondered
     that there was none to uphold:
Therefore mine own arm brought salvation . . .
     and my fury upheld me.

I will mention the loving kindness of the Lord . . .
     for He said,
Surely they are my people . . .: So He was their Saviour.

From both the second part of this psalm and from Jesus'
own last words from the Cross, it would seem that the
agony of the Dereliction passed and that His serenity
returned before His Spirit's departure.

As He girded Himself to enter Sheol for the final conflict
and the victory, He gave His spirit into the Father's keeping
with His accustomed confidence,

> For He hath not despised nor abhorred the affliction
>   of the afflicted (One),
> neither hath he hid his face from him;
> but when he cried unto him, he heard. (v. 24).

The final note is of peace and victory;

> They shall come and shall declare His righteousness
>   unto a people that shall be born, that He
>   hath done this.

In Psalm 22 may be discerned the whole gamut of feeling
scaled by Jesus during those hours on the Cross, from the
awful depths of horror and woe, to peace, hope, and
sublime gladness, as He meditates —

> My praise shall be of Thee in the great
>   congregation . . .
> All the ends of the world shall remember
>   and turn unto the Lord:
> And all the kindreds of the nations shall
>   worship before Thee. (vs. 25-27).

The joy of that day is described in the 5th chapter of
Revelation:

> And they sang a new song, saying . . . Blessing, and
>   honour, and glory, and power, be unto
>   Him that sitteth upon the throne, and unto
>   the Lamb for ever and ever.

The voices thus raised are those whom 'Thou hast
redeemed out of every kindred, and tongue, and people,

and nation'. By the sacrifice on the Cross the 'vox humana' is added to the harmony of the angelic choir, bringing to fruition the final prophecy of this psalm.

PSALM 23.

This psalm is so dear to us as an expression of our own spiritual experience that it is hard to look at it differently. But if we can continue our exploration of Jesus' thoughts, we shall find that the Shepherd Psalm fits into their sequence precisely where it is, between the agony of Calvary in Psalm 22 and the glory of the Ascension in Psalm 24.

The horror of great darkness has given way to calm and peace. Hope and even joy were His while He was yet on the Cross, and the last words, 'Into Thy hands I commit my spirit' must have been spoken with confidence. It is exactly on this note that Psalm 23 is composed, and an exploration in this light will be rewarding.

Though the believer quite rightly thinks of Jesus as the Good Shepherd Himself, and the metaphor of the Shepherd caring for His sheep runs through His ministry right on to the period after the resurrection when He desires Peter to feed His sheep and His lambs, it would not be out of place to attribute this psalm also to Jesus' thoughts on His own relationship with the Father. God was known as the 'Shepherd of Israel'. Jesus had committed His soul to God's keeping. For us that would mean the moment of our soul's departure to be with Christ. But *His* precious soul had a task to fulfill before He could go to His Father. It was the culminating point of His whole purpose in becoming Man. We have little information, if any, about these moments. He had defeated Satan's wiles at every turn during His lifetime on earth and He accomplished the redemption of man by going to the Cross and dying there the Innocent Victim of God's Justice. Thus He had purchased eternal life for all who believe in Him. But His work was not yet complete. (Now that He ascended, what is it but that) He also descended first into the lower parts of the earth. (Eph. 4:9).

He must carry the battle to the very seat of Satan's kingdom, and there He must wrest from the enemy's clutches all those who had died in faith. He must break the bondage of death and tear down the portals of the stronghold of Satan so that never more should its power hold any believer. This greater than Samson carried the gate of the enemy to the top of the hill. He pulled down the pillars of Hades and destroyed a greater enemy by His death than by His life. It was for that part of His mission that He commended His soul to the Father's keeping. He need not have spoken these words, otherwise, because His soul, once released from the body, would of its own nature have returned immediately Home.

Now this Shepherd Psalm pictures what may have been His feelings as He prepared to enter the realm of Satan's dominion. He commended His soul to the keeping of God as His Shepherd and therefore He could walk through the valley of the shadow of death and fear no evil because God was with Him. The thought of God's Presence comforts Him. His peace of mind is such now that it compares with resting in green pastures by still waters. What a contrast with the cry a few hours earlier of 'I thirst!'. He could also say that God had prepared a table before Him in the presence of His enemies. He would gather the waiting souls in Sheol as an abundant harvest, see the travail of His soul, and be satisfied. His cup would run over with joy as He presented them, redeemed, to His Father (as Samson did the honey from the lion he had torn), and then, His soul restored to the body in resurrection, He would dwell in the house of the Lord for ever.

So this psalm, like a piece into a mosaic, exactly fits this period in the experience of our Saviour and falls precisely into the position necessary to complete another section of His spiritual history which would otherwise never have been told, since it took place beyond the range of human witness.

PSALM 24.

This is the third of the great trio of Psalms covering the

93

Passion of our Lord: Psalm 22 gives Jesus' thoughts while on the Cross; Psalm 23 His meditation in the silent moments when He was preparing to leave this world, and Psalm 24 tells of His resurrection and reception into the Father's Presence.

There are two parts to this psalm, and 'Lift up your heads, ye gates', is the second. At first verses 1-6 do not seem to be part of the same thought, and the break in the continuity both of tone and theme would suggest two separate psalms. Yet they are one in the experience of the Lord Jesus.

Taking our clue from the second half, and assigning it to the Ascension (as many teachers have done), the first part naturally belongs to the Resurrection. Thus both parts of this psalm give expression to His thoughts as He returned victorious, first to this earth in His glorified body, and then to His heavenly abode as Conqueror and King.

Let us examine the possibilities of verses 1 to 6 in this light. It is the hour of early dawn on Easter morning. Jesus' soul has been absent in the dark regions of Sheol where He has fought and vanquished its terrible prince, and now His Spirit has returned to the waiting body and He has come out of the tomb.

Imagine what His thoughts must have been as He surveyed the garden, the countryside, and in His mind, the whole earth! Redeemed! 'Having made peace through the blood of His cross, by Him to reconcile all things unto Himself'. (Col. 1:20). It was done! No more mockery and spitting; the Cross lay behind Him, and His spirit rejoiced, triumphant and overflowing with divine love for the world of man whose redemption He had bought at so great a price. 'The earth is the LORD'S' . . .

The words of David's psalm in II Sam. 23 vividly reflect the scene as Jesus rose, bringing life from the dead. It was Spring in Palestine and he saw it haloed with the mystic glory of a new day; new life was springing forth all around. His heart exultant at the victory over the Evil One beheld His world, in the light of a new creation. Perhaps the darkness that descended on Calvary had burst out in a terrible storm; rain-washed and touched by the first rays of the rising sun early on the first day of the week, the surroundings sparkled with myriad gems, and the Sun of Righteousness Himself arose, shining forth resplendently. David describes it:

> And He shall be as the light of the morning, when the
>   sun riseth; even a morning without clouds;
> As the tender grass springing out of the earth by clear
>   shining after rain. (II Sam. 23:4).

A morning without clouds! clear shining after rain! that must have been the sensation of Jesus physically and spiritually as He beheld His beloved land on that first moment of His resurrection. And the Psalmist puts His thoughts into words in the opening lines of Psalm 24:

> The earth is the Lord's and the fulness thereof;
> The world, and they that dwell therein.

He had broken the power of Satan; He had redeemed the earth and man that dwells therein. They were the Lord's in a new and remarkable relationship; a man need never again despair at the curse! How glorious it all must have looked to Him! What joy must have filled His exultant heart as He looked about in that first instant!

We know it is He because here again is the particular feature by which He is identified. It is the Righteous Man of Psalm 1 —

> Who shall ascend unto the hill of the Lord?
> Or who shall stand in His holy place?
> He that hath clean hands and a pure heart;
> Who hath not lifted up his soul unto vanity,
>   nor sworn deceitfully.

I am the way, the truth and the life, He had told His disciples. He now bore witness to the truth of His claim. He had brought life. He was the True and Living Way.

The Psalm continues:

> He shall receive blessing from the Lord, . . .
> This is the generation of them that seek Him.

'Touch me not', He told Mary in that Resurrection garden, 'for I have not yet ascended to my Father . . . Go to my brethren and say unto them, I ascend unto my Father and your Father; to my God and your God'. This was the new generation, His blood-bought blood-begot children.

It seems rather strange that v. 6 should end '. . . that seek thy face O Jacob. Selah'. The address to Jacob surprises, for the sense of the previous verse obviously points to the Just One, and that it is the Lord whose face they seek. In certain psalms, as in the Messianic 129th, the sufferer is referred to as 'Israel' ('The plowers plowed upon my back' . . .) The meditative pause indicated here by the 'Selah' that follows, infers that a deeper thought lies below the surface. 'Jacob' the nation was God's Chosen People. The Just One described in verses 4 and 5 is God's Chosen One, the Messiah, God's Christ, and in the context which we are exploring, 'Jacob' is more apt than 'Israel', since it is not as Prince that he has been presented but rather as the One substituting.

Now come the famous exclamations, like a fanfare of trumpets announcing the King's ceremonial arrival:

> Lift up your heads, O ye gates,
> and be ye lift up, ye everlasting doors;
> And the King of Glory shall come in.

There follows the challenge and answer in dramatic form: the sentry demanding the password. It is given, and the 'Lord, strong and mighty, the Lord mighty in battle, the Lord of hosts' sweeps through the holy portals, with, surely the redeemed souls delivered from Sheol triumphantly in His train.

This ringing address to the gates to be lifted for the entry of the King of Glory has often been ascribed to the Ascension scene which we read in the first Chapter of Acts, when our Lord left this earth in bodily presence and ascended to Heaven. But indeed there was an earlier one. When Jesus told Mary not to touch Him because He had not yet ascended to the Father, He did not infer that he was going to wait forty days before doing so. 'I ascend . . .'

infers that he is about to do so immediately after, and in fact later He offered His hands and His side to be handled by Thomas. So this triumphal entry told of in the Psalm must have taken place on that wonderful Resurrection morning, on the first Easter Day.

> 'And I saw,' says Daniel, in the night visions, and behold, one like the Son of Man came with the clouds of heaven, and came to the Ancient of Days, and they brought him near before him, and there was given him dominion, and glory, and a kingdom .. ; his dominion is an everlasting dominion, which shall not pass away, and his kingdom that which shall not be destroyed. (Dan. 7:13,14).

There were two 'enterings', hence the repeated question, one on His reporting immediately after the Resurrection (seen by Daniel); the second, witnessed by the apostles (Acts 1) being forty days later.

Though the great 24th psalm may well be David's song for the bringing of the Ark of the Covenant to Jerusalem (II Sam. 6:12-19), it clearly fits in as a marvellous culmination to this trio of Messianic psalms.

PSALM 25.

The unusual opening line of Psalm 25 —

> Unto Thee, O Lord, do I lift up my soul,

conveys that this is a soul's deep converse with his God. Other psalms speak of lifting up clean hands or the suppliant's eyes (cf. v. 15 of this psalm) to God, but here the author lifts up his soul, as in that great messianic psalm of David, the 86th, v. 4, which shares several other points with this one, as does also Psalm 143. The tone is intimate communing with God as with a loved and trusted Friend, and reveals confidence in His goodness, mercy, and loving kindness, as the speaker contemplates the charateristics of His relationship with those who seek to know His way.

Yet surprisingly enough, the psalmist also includes prayers for pardon. Some of the later psalms in this BOOK I, notably 31, 38 and 40, which among petitions for help and guidance, confess sin and pray for pardon, contain nevertheless verses which point significantly to the experiences of Christ (cf. 31:5; 38:11; 40:6). Thus a link with the Suffering Servant is clearly established. But no obvious pointers in this psalm identify the Sinless One as the suppliant for forgiveness, unless it be v. 20, 'O keep my soul', recalling as it does the last cry from the Cross.

There are in this psalm certain statements that can in no way form part of Christ's thoughts and personal experience, notably v. 7 — 'Remember not the sins of my youth, nor my transgressions'. Christ knew no sin until the burden of the world's iniquity was laid upon Him for expiation. Again in v. 11 — 'Pardon mine iniquity for it is great', but this petition is not embedded in anguish as in Psalm 38 where it is more easily associated with the expiation on Calvary. The same objection applies to v. 18, 'forgive all my sins'.

It must be acknowledged, however, that but for these three verses, the psalm might be thought of as expressing a prayer of the Righteous One. We have been seeking to trace a portrait by assuming not only that all the psalms of David portray the Messiah but that the Holy Ghost guided the order in which they should be placed when BOOK I was put together. The first cycle of the story has been completed with the Ascension. This then must open a new series. By close scrutiny it should be possible to find out if this, too, adds to the Portrait. Since the scenes cannot continue chronologically, and the emotional and structural climax has already been reached (psalms 22-24), it may be that these enlarge on occasions previously inferred.

On examination there are found in Psalm 25 more parallels with the life and character of the Saviour than were at first evident. Jesus would and did often in the messianic psalms lift up His heart to God for spiritual sustenance and succour (v. 1,2). He also asked that God's way be shown to Him and explicitly declared His dependence upon God for guidance (v. 4,5).

> Lead me in Thy truth . . , On Thee do I
> wait all the day.

He also spoke of Himself as meek, and recommended
meekness to His followers (v. 9):

> The meek will He guide in judgment; the
> meek will He teach His way.

Compare Mat. 11:28. Again, there is the metaphor of the
'net', v. 5, which the enemy has set to ensnare Him, a figure
which often occurs in the messianic psalms (31:4; 35:8); and
also the prayer to God to bring him out of his distress (v.
17) and Psalms 31:15; 34:4; 35:17; 40:2. There is the
pathetic complaint of unmerited hatred directed against
him. Most of all, 'O keep my soul' (v. 20) echoes the last
Word from the Cross of Psalm 31:5, and the words
'integrity' and 'uprightness' seem to indicate the speaker
who is in 'distress', 'troubles' and 'affliction'.

Even in the axiom-like verses, characteristic of the
acrostic psalms, there are sufficient similarities to indicate a
close connection with Messianic thought, especially that of
confidence in the justice and faithfulness of God (v. 6); His
goodness (v. 8); and the promise of guidance and peace to
those that fear Him (v. 10-15). But the final petition seems
not to be of this connection:

> Redeem Israel, O God, out of all his troubles.

But we have the clue in v. 6 of the previous psalm. The
psalmist has composed a prayer as spoken by Israel. The
nation itself is impersonated by the Messiah, as is 'Jacob' in
Psalm 24:5.

Certain other points offer rich inferences which reward
examination. verse 4 — Show me, teach me, lead me; guide
v. 9. It is deeply moving to realize that so did the Lord
humble Himself, being Man, that He felt the need of God's
guidance at every stage. Though He thought it not robbery
to be equal with God, even He did not presume to speak or
act without the Father's express will, as He implied in John
10:26-29; 10:18. It is therefore not unlikely, according to vs.

4,5,9 of this psalm, that Jesus would pray God to show Him both what He wished Him to do and when it should be done. This would be part of the human condition which He accepted, having 'divested Himself' (French, S'est dépouillé lui même) of His divine prerogative. He stripped Himself and took upon Him the form of a servant . . . and being found in fashion as a man he humbled himself and became obedient unto death. (Phil. 2:7,8).

But 'sins', 'iniquity', 'transgressions' — these are not to be spoken of and cannot at all be associated with the holy Son of God. And yet, when the sins of the world were laid upon Him and 'He was *made sin* for us', may not the psalmist's words be His as He declares them, paying for that which He had not taken, praying for pardon while in the very act of expiating them? Thus the setting for this psalm in relation to the experience of Jesus is the hour when darkness veiled the scene, for here also is the verse which became the final cry from the Cross.

Finally, there is the allusion to 'the sins of my youth'. This is an admission of the speaker's own sin and cannot be Christ's in any concept. He knew no sin. His position was not that of the believer who, looking back on his youth, realizes that certain acts done in innocence were in fact sinful, for He knew all along what was pure and right and holy.

Discipline, however, is part of life, especially during youth, and we are told both that He 'grew' and that He 'learned'. His determination at the age of twelve to be about His Father's business immediately is told in His first recorded words. Having reached the age of responsibility before the Law, the Holy Child may have thought He need not remain subject to His earthly guardians but was free to follow His own initiative. Of royal birth and perfectly endowed, He had a commanding and energetic nature, and it was bent to the one purpose of carrying out the task for which He had come. He perhaps had to learn that (v. 9) 'The *meek* will He guide .. ; the meek will He teach' . . . The Evangelist records that He developed like every human child, from youth to maturity. We may ponder whether the reference to youth may indicate that He did not fully realize at first that in His earthly environment He had to await the

Father's signal with regard to the time and manner in which His work was to begin. 'Ye have need of patience' might have been one of the lessons He had to learn. Though not a sin, His zealous reply to his mother could have appeared retrospectively to His more mature understanding as revealing a youthful independence of spirit, even impetuousness, which He never again permitted Himself.

By the time he received His heavenly Father's commission to go forth He had exercised Himself in submission and meekness. His public deference to His Father's will was later often emphasized, underlining the importance to Him of the early experience that taught it. In heaven His mind and the Father's were One. It was only in the flesh — a new environment, as it were — that He would have to learn to await orders. He voluntarily placed Himself under such limitations when He said, 'Lo, I come . . . to do Thy will, O God'. It is conceivable that He had to find out by experience all that was implied in the being 'made in the likeness of men'. How marvellous and moving to our hearts is the thought that He, too, had to wait God's time with faith and patience.

Verses 8-10, 12-14 of this psalm seem more appropriate to meditation than prayer:

All the paths of the Lord are mercy and truth. (v. 10).
The secret of the Lord is with them that fear Him. (v. 14).

Yet these sayings form part of the prayer, for they are axioms of the Upright Man of Psalm 1, who meditates continually in God's Law. They identify the Speaker of the prayer: His 'eyes are ever toward the Lord' (v. 15). In His desolation and affliction He prays to be brought out of His distress (v. 17). The prayer, 'O keep my soul', of v. 20, is akin to the last words of the Crucified as He prepared to give up His Spirit, committing Himself to the Father's keeping. The touching petition of v. 17, with the closing words of the Psalm (v. 22), are His plea for the resurrection of His body —

> O bring me out of my distress . . .
> O keep my soul and deliver me, for I put my
> trust in Thee —

So purely and totally had He taken upon Himself man's condition. But He was the Righteous Man, God's own Son, for He can add the claim of His fulfilment of His part in the Covenant —

> Let integrity and uprightness preserve me,
> for I wait on Thee —

even there, He waited upon God to give the command, showing His complete obedience as well as His trust. His final prayer is on behalf of the purpose for which He had come: Redemption.

Thus, as it unfolds, this psalm may well testify to the workings of Jesus' thoughts as He remained outwardly silent in that most solemn hour on the Cross, the final moments of His earthly life.

PSALM 26.

If this psalm is read as only a poem by David, it will appear presumptuous on his part to claim integrity in the sight of God by his own righteousness and virtue of his own merits. But if we see it within the larger framework of the portrait of the Redeemer which, though often hidden is present in all David's psalms, we recognize here at once the Righteous Man of Psalms 1 and 15. The words of this psalm then do not presume because their true author is God's Chosen One, and belong to that other plane — the mind of Jesus.

In Psalms such as this one the human writer has been lifted out of himself and the limitations of personal experience, to the sublime position of the sinless Christ, and he writes in the spirit of a life of flawless integrity. David was an upright man and feared his God, loved and sought to serve Him, but when he failed in one point and committed a grievous sin, he could not and never did lay claim to righteousness. The consequences of his act were ever before him. The psalm makes much more sense and vindicates every protestation of innocence therein if we take it as a meditation or prayer of the Righteous Man, and it may well express His thoughts as He walked in the Temple precincts after clearing out the money-changers.

The statements are more emphatic here than in Psalms 1 and 15 because here they are in the first person, and whereas David might contemplate that Just and Perfect Man in the 3rd person, it is most unlikely that David would attribute these qualities to himself, for he was anything but self-righteous. Hence we have here words that may voice Jesus' own thoughts about Himself.

He has come to the place of worship, the Father's House on earth, and in His presence the Son can state unhesitatingly:

> I have walked in mine integrity . . .
> I have walked in Thy truth.

and He can stand before that awful Presence with His heart laid open to the scrutiny of God and invite Him to see for Himself —

> Judge me, O Lord; . . . Examine me, O Lord;
>   and prove me
> Try my reins and my heart.

We have considered in Psalm 22 how Jesus kept Himself unspotted that He might offer His unblemished life to God in sacrifice. In the light of this, we sense here a holy joy as He stands before God and swears to His absolute purity. Perhaps the thought of Himself as the Lamb of God may have come to Him as He beheld the altar there. He affirms His refusal to associate with vain persons or with dissemblers. He has —

> . . . hated the congregation of evil doers
> and will not sit with the wicked.

It is the same imagery as that of Psalm 1, but here the context seems to point to a real event. Still panting from His exertions with the whip of cords and His blood stirred with anger at the men who had turned His Father's house into a den of thieves, He had not dissembled His indignation.

> In their hands is mischief, and their right hand
> is full of bribes.

They were there unmolested because they had probably bribed the High Priest or some other dignitary, He would not even 'go in' with these dissembling money-makers crowding the precincts.

Having cleared the Temple of all the merchandise and overturned the money tables, He vindicates His act before God and 'washes (His) hands in innocency' — perhaps at the laver — so in proper decorum and quietude He can 'compass thine altar, O Lord, and publish with the voice of thanksgiving . . . all Thy wondrous works.'

With regard to 'I will compass Thine altar', David Baron tells how this was done, *Types, Psalms and Prophecies* —

> 'On the 7th day of the Feast of Tabernacles the people all carried long palm branches. The choir of Levites commenced to sing the Hallel (Psalm 113-118). Soon the whole crowd, led by the priests, marched in procession round the altar, encompassing it seven times. As the singers reached the words, 'Blessed is He that cometh in the name of the Lord' (118:26) the people joined in the words, waved their palm branches and accompanied the song with loud exclamations of joy.' And see also *The Ancient Scriptures and the Modern Jew*, by the same author.

Here we may add the poignant reminder of the verse that follows, and think how it affected the human Christ as He almost certainly joined in with the throng encompassing the altar: 'Bind the sacrifice with cords, even unto the horns of the altar . . .' Verily, for it was the cords of Love and Obedience which should bind Him there.

Now the Just Man (as though justifying His cleansing of the Temple) addresses His God:

> Lord, I have loved the habitation of Thy house,
> and the place where Thine honour dwelleth.

He prays God to keep Him from an untimely death —

> Gather not my soul with sinners, nor my life
> with bloody men.

and as though reaffirming His identity the opening words are repeated:

> As for me, I will walk in mine integrity.

Note that v. 11, 'I have walked'. Now He can say —

> My foot standeth in an even place . . .
> in the congregation will I bless the Lord.

One wonders if the words 'their hands are full of bribes' suggest an added reason for His terrible anger. When He ordered the merchants out, did they offer Him (this zealous rabbi!) a portion of their ill-gotten gains that they might be allowed to stay? The fury behind the whip was the measure of the Righteous Man's indignation.

PSALM 27.

An outline of the contents of this psalm shows:

Expressions of confidence in God's protection. (vs. 1-6).

Abrupt change of tone, a plea for mercy and succour. vs. (7;-2).

Return to equanimity and confidence; encouragement in the Lord. (vs. 13,14).

Several topics to be examined arise:

a. the probable reason for the sudden change of tone from confidence to fear, from 'I will sing' (v. 6) to 'when I cry' (v. 7).

b. the probable occasion in Jesus' experience to which these emotions are suited.

c. the significance of the brief dialogue of v. 8 —

Seek ye my face. Thy face, Lord, will I seek.

The answer to a. may be simply one of structure: the psalm is constructed on dramatic lines, the opening and close being in the present time of its composition, and the parenthetical middle passage of pleading for safety being the occasion that brought forth the psalm; the whole forming a circular movement ending where it began, in peace and confidence. Or the author is standing on the brink of some great and dangerous enterprise. He has reason to fear, but is convinced that in the time of trouble God will deliver him.

By gathering up several clues throughout the middle section particularly, we may arrive at an occasion when the phrases express an actual occurence in the life of Jesus. Take v. 2 —

When mine enemies and my foes came,
they stumbled and fell.

John tells us (18:5,6): As soon as He had said unto them, I am (He), they went backward and fell to the ground. There are 'enemies', 'foes', 'the wicked' (v. 2); 'a host', v. 3; and in Matt. 26:47 — 'with him (Judas) a great multitude with swords and staves'.

. . . false witnesses are risen up against me. (v. 12);

and in Mark 14:56. For many bear false witness against him.

All of these references in different Gospels, are from the account of the night of Jesus' arrest. The experiences of that night are here presented within a framework of His habitual confidence and strength in the upholding power of God. The fragment of dialogue gives the secret clue, His constant communion with God, 'my light, my salvation, the strength of my life.' He cried (v. 9) —

Leave me not, O God of my salvation.

The secret reassurance came (as to Jeremiah, Jer. 1:8) 'Seek ye my face'. His heart responded, 'Thy face, Lord, will I seek'. God had said, Be not afraid of their faces; keep your eyes on me', and so, by keeping His gaze on the Father's countenance not on the foes around, His equanimity was preserved, (v. 13) —

I had fainted unless I had believed to see the goodness of the Lord in the land of the living.

Perhaps the inner dialogue took place between Jesus and the Father when the mob burst into the garden to arrest Him, and in answer to His cry for help (v. 7), 'Have mercy upon me, and answer me'.

But what was His fear? Why should He cry thus? He knew that 'the Son of man must be lifted up'. He was prepared for it and knew, besides that His hour had come, for He had said so. There is a special circumstance that explains and justifies this and the further cry in v. 9 — 'Leave me not, neither forsake me, O God of my salvation'.

Jesus knew His life to be most precious in the sight of God because He was to lay it down of His own will, an offering for the sins of the world. There was, humanly speaking, a very real danger that it would be taken by violence, for He knew that the devil wanted above all to prevent that holy, willing Sacrifice from reaching the altar, and Redemption from being consummated. This psalm is therefore not the expression of a faint heart fearful of death, but is a passionate intercession for the preservation of a holy treasure that belonged to God. He would be preserved and

In the secret of His tabernacle shall He hide me;
And now shall my head be lifted up
Above mine enemies round about me.

'. . .And I, if I be lifted up, I will draw all men unto me', He said. This He said, signifying what death He should die.

107

(John 12:32,33).

The number of those seeking to destroy His life was already great, perhaps not because they hated Him personally but because He openly challenged the validity of 'the commandments of men' (Mark 7:7-13. Mat. 15:9). Beginning by healing the man's withered hand on a Sabbath in the synagogue, He allowed His disciples to pluck and eat corn on the Sabbath, and even to have a meal without washing themselves. On these and other occasions He had triumphantly overriden the authority of the scribes; hence He knew that their anger would increase and be very fierce. He casts Himself upon God:

> Though an host should encamp against me, my
>   heart shall not fear,
> Though war should rise against me, in this will I
>   be confident.
> One thing have I desired of the Lord, that will I
>   seek after:
> That I may dwell in the house of the Lord
>   all the days of my life,
> To behold the beauty of the Lord, and to inquire
>   at His temple.

It is true that this, one of David's most lovely requests, beautifully voices our own heart's prayer. But we may think that the Saviour also had desired of His God that one thing, that, His mission fulfilled, He would as Psalm 23 puts it, dwell in the house of the Lord for ever in His human form.

There is a pendulum movement throughout this psalm, with expressions of devotion and joy in the Lord interspersed with petitions for protection from His enemies; perhaps the latter denotes a natural human fear, but when He says —
And now shall my head be lifted up above mine enemies (v. 6) it is the divine mind of the Christ seeing all men drawn unto God. His enemies who raged about Him did not know that precisely the laying down of His life was what He had come to do. 'No man taketh it from me, I lay it down of myself', He said. (John 10:18). When He was 'lifted up', it would be the fulfilling of God's purpose and thus signify not defeat at the hands of men but victory for

the designs of God.

Therefore will I offer in His tabernacle sacrifices of Joy (v. 6). His holy joy is inspired by assurances and thanksgiving. The offering was to be made 'with rejoicing and with singing, as it was ordained by David' (II Chron. 23:18). It is in this context that the psalmist announces, 'I will sing, yea, I will sing praises unto the Lord'. Before Jesus, 'knowing all things that should come upon Him, went out', He had 'sung an hymn' (Mark 14:26). Secretly, His heart rejoiced. But in those turbulent moments of the arrest, He may well have made His own the prayer, 'Leave me not, neither forsake me. O God of my salvation'. How deeply moving is the thought that in the final issue He would have to be forsaken even after this plea!

But for the last two verses, the rest of the psalm continues in the strain of petitions for personal safety:

> Deliver me not unto the will of mine enemies,
> for false witnesses are risen up against me,
> and such as breathe out cruelty.

The reference to false witnesses, as we have seen, can be linked with the night of the arrest and the accusations before Pilate. The prayer for deliverance is His urgent plea that God's plan be not frustrated at the last, for the only charge they could legally bring was that He spoke of God as His Father, thus 'making Himself equal with God', and the penalty of the law for blasphemy was stoning to death. Had this taken place, His blood would not have been shed as the Lamb of God, and neither would the Body have been presented for sacrifice with no bone broken. As He was dragged along under arrest, surrounded by men thirsting for His death, He may have encouraged Himself in the Lord in the words of the last verse:

> . . . be of good courage and He shall strengthen
>   thine heart.
> Wait, I say, on the Lord.

The repetition of the phrase suggests the urgency of the moment and the heroic firmness which met it.

What a touching insight into His heart during those silent moments is obtained by thus applying this 27th psalm to His experience on that fateful night! Depending on God for endurance to carry out His purposes to the last jot, He sees the threat of danger to His Person as a potential frustration of that Plan, but His divine Spirit is as ever, perfectly in tune with His Father. The pendulum movement proves to be an artistic device for working on two planes at once.

It is interesting to note that in verses 4-6 there are several synonyms for God's dwelling: House of the Lord, His temple, His pavilion, His tabernacle. This 'Tabernacle' was Jesus' Body. We have noted that the injunction was to 'offer sacrifices of joy *in His tabernacle.*'

☆   ☆   ☆

PSALM 28.

Like the preceding one, this psalm seems to give utterance to the silent cry from the heart of the Messiah after the arrest in Gethsemane; and if Psalm 27 expresses His thoughts during the arrest, Psalm 28 gives them as He was being led away by His captors. His cry to heaven is for strength and spiritual support in this hour so dark that it suggests the 'pit' of death. He cries to God as the rock for His feet to stand upon, and prays Him for a word —

Be not silent unto me: lest, if thou be silent unto me,
I become like them that go down into the pit.

Communication between Him and the Father was always freely exercised, His Father's voice audible in His heart at all times. It is when we realize this that we come in some measure to apprehend the agony of desolation at the dereliction when suddenly that Voice ceased. The one horror He here prays to be spared is of God's silence at the supreme moment; if the comfort of His Presence be withheld His death would be that of the damned. The repetition emphasizes the urgency of the plea once again: Be not silent unto me, lest if thou be silent . . .

As He was forced at a smart pace up the road to the city, hustled by the rabble, He prays — 'Draw me not away with the wicked . . . Mischief is in their heart'. Well He knew it. Without bitterness yet how naturally human is the sentiment of v. 4 in this connection —

Give them according to their deed, and according
to the wickedness of their endeavours —

and yet He healed the ear struck off an enemy by His friend. The evil they were doing at the moment was not the arrest of a man, it was a concentrated effort to do away with the Truth.

Give them after the work of their hands;
render to them their desert,

the verse continues. this is not vindictiveness, for the Son of man goeth as it is written of Him, but woe unto that man by whom He is betrayed! (Matt. 26:24). They should receive their deserts because:

They regard not the works of the Lord;
nor the operation of His hands.

Miracles of healing, miracles of feeding, miracles of grace, yet they had refused to recognize them as signs of God's Hand. Then God shall destroy them. This gives the clue by which to understand the rightness of these imprecations. They are not hurled against the ignorant but against those that wilfully oppose God's grace.

The turning point of the psalm comes here. The answer has come; He must have received reassurance from the Father for He gives thanks:

Blessed be the Lord, because He hath heard the voice
of my supplications.

Even as His heart cried, it was strengthened by the loved Voice and now He can go forward with calm control to face the mock tribunal and the real one, and hold His peace.

The agony and the tears are left behind; now He can say:

The Lord is my strength and my shield;
My heart trusted in Him, and I am helped;
Therefore my heart greatly rejoiceth;
And with my song will I praise Him.

Again that song in the night! That cry of fear or loneliness or weakness always turns to glad song as His prayer is instantly and secretly answered. His composure is not Olympian indifference: it is divine and God-given peace. As He goes back over the brook Kedron, having asked that His disciples be allowed to go free, back through the City gate and along the dark streets, bound, to the house of Annas, father-in-law to the High Priest, in His heart He is singing:

The Lord . . . is the saving strength of His Anointed. Here is His identity! It is God's Anointed. He had almost fainted when He asked that the Cup pass from Him, but now He has received saving strength and knows He will not fail but will be upheld until all is accomplished. The end of His mission lies immediately before Him as He prays —

Save thy people, and bless thine inheritance.
Feed them also, and lift them up for ever.

If we now recapitulate we shall see what has been added to the Portrait of Jesus from these psalms.

In the first place what emerges is the quality of His character. As the last year of His sojourn on earth dwindled into months and weeks He pressed forward purposefully, eagerly, to accomplish that for which He had been sent. In the words of Paul, He pressed toward the mark for the prize of the high calling of God. He seems to have lived constantly on two planes at once; on the human one conscious of physical danger and on the divine in the cognisance of His destiny in the act of Redemption.

That a man should orient his life towards the immolation of himself is not natural from the human point of view; yet that is what we find our Saviour doing, and doing with joy. The motive force which dominated His life on earth was the accomplishment of His Father's will. To do this He was in constant dependence upon God for strength and fortitude, and seems to have felt His human frailty though aware of His divine uniqueness as the Lamb of God. He must offer a flawless character and a body without blemish, and there is a holy joy in doing so. In fact, by the guidance of these psalms it can be stated that as the awful hour approached His joy increased.

Each day that went by, the tension of the conflict grew and the risk was greater that His life might be snatched by fanatic hands before the time. It must have been a relief to enter the last week and to know that the Passover was approaching. This feeling is confirmed in His own words recorded by Luke (12:50), 'I have a baptism to be baptized with; and how am I straightened till it be accomplished!'

In a word, what marked the third year of His public career most significantly was a steadfastness with joy as He directed His steps to the consummation of His task. His spirit was not a whit less eager than at the beginning.

PSALM 29.

We may well wonder at what part of our Lord's career this magnificent Psalm became most apt. It has been remarked that it 'Opens with Gloria in Excelsis and closes with Pax in Terris.' It is one of the world's greatest poems, in which during a significant manifestation of God's majesty and power in a rending of the skies, the poet's heart is not cowed but spurred to exult at the grandeur of His voice. Such a poem rises far above a Byron's ecstatic response to the reverberations of thunder in the Alps, for the latter concludes with a cry wrung from the author's frailty. With what telling simplicity the psalmist has achieved so much greater an effect!

It is a Psalm sung at the Jewish festival in commemoration of the giving of the Law on Sinai; and surely the thunder and lightenings as expressive of the awful voice of God but concluding in Peace were never so strikingly described. At

Sinai the 'glory like a devouring fire' gave place to the serenity of the vision of the God of Israel in Whose Presence the people 'did eat and drink'. (Exod. 19 and 24).

There were storms, no doubt, during the lifetime of our Lord. Those we are told of generally emphasize the wind and its effect on the Lake of Galilee. If we try to see this psalm as it might have sprung to the mind of Jesus during a literal storm on land, we must agree that no such manifestation of God's power is recorded. The convulsions of this violent thunderstorm associate it with the terrible on the plane of the divine. A vivid picture of the forces of nature, its real meaning lies in the significant metaphors.

Glorious and admirable though God's might is to the heart of His followers, it should not be forgotten that it has power to destroy and is terrible, as Moses so often reminded Israel at Sinai. In the imagery of the Psalm, it breaks even the great cedars of Lebanon and shakes the mountains. Only the Righteous Man can contemplate this spectacle of power without a qualm. Let the mighty thunder and the cleaving lightning — it seems to say — remind man of the power of His glory and let man therefore render homage to Him with a pure heart in the beauty of holiness.

On earth Jesus could appreciate as never before the effect on man of great atmospheric displays. They engender awe and speak of the Almighty's power firmly holding them in His grasp and yet able to unleash them upon puny man, showing how terrible is His holiness.

> The Lord sitteth upon the flood;
> yea, the Lord sitteth King for ever —

and from the Throne on high He sends not destruction to His people but PEACE. Couched in poetic imagery of thunder, lightning and tearing wind, the reference is to the Voice of God and His Presence at the giving of the Law on Sinai. Although Lebanon is named twice, and the rushing torrents speak more of Hermon than the environs of Jerusalem, the poet's main theme is 'the voice of the Lord that thunders . . . is powerful . . . breaketh the cedars . . . divideth the flames of fire . . . shaketh the wilderness . . . discovereth the forests . . . and in His temple doth every one speak of His glory.'

There was no 'temple' properly speaking in David's time. (This is entitled 'A Psalm of David'); nor are we told of any fierce manifestations of God's Presence in Shiloh when David brought the Ark of the Covenant to the tent he had pitched for it in the 'city of David' (I Chron. 15,16). Hence David is not necessarily writing about an event he personally witnessed. It is his radiant poetic vision which directs this prince to celebrate the great starting-point of God's revelation of Himself to the whole nation. Exodus ch. 19 and Deut. ch. 5 give the account in a narrative less vibrant than David's exultant psalm but the same graphic imagery is used to describe the signs of God's Presence:

> There were thunders and lightnings . . . and the voice of a trumpet exceeding loud so that the people . . . trembled . . . and the Lord descended . . and the whole mount quaked greatly . . . and the trumpet waxed louder and louder . . . and God answered by a voice . . .

In Moses' personal account in his oration of Deut. 4 the 'Voice' is more frequently mentioned and this seems to be the passage in the psalmist's mind. The 'temple' in the psalm is the poetic image of the heights of heaven, and prophetically it points to the temple of which Haggai was speaking: The desire of all nations shall come; and I will fill this house (i.e. the rebuilt Temple after the captivity) with glory, saith the Lord of hosts: The glory of this latter house shall be greater than the former, saith the Lord of hosts, and in this place will I give peace.

We behold the fulfilment of Haggai's prophecy when the Lord Jesus Himself stood in that same temple on the day when the giving of the Law was remembered and celebrated. It is easy to imagine that this very psalm may have been sung by Him then and on other occasions every year. How familiar to Him was the fact that 'in His temple doth everyone speak of His glory' (v. 19). For in spite of the terribleness of the Voice and the awfulness of the Presence that gave the Law, the personal message to Israel then as now was Mercy and the Covenant of Peace. (v. 11).

☆　　☆　　☆

PSALM 30.

Rightly or not, the title given to this Psalm is 'A Song at the dedication of the house of David'. It is an expression of gratitude to God after the author has undergone some very great crisis in which he has faced death, has cried out to God, and been saved:

> I cried unto Thee and Thou hast healed me (v. 2).
> Thou hast brought my soul out of the grave:
> Thou hast kept me alive . . . (v. 3).
>
> His anger endureth but a moment . . .
> Joy cometh in the morning. (v .5).
> Thou didst hide Thy face and I was troubled. (v. 7).
>
> . . . Lord, be Thou my helper. (v. 10)
>
> Thou hast turned my mourning into dancing (v. 11).
> I will give thanks unto Thee for ever. (v. 12).

To the Messiah whose soul was 'kept alive'; who bore God's anger and from Whom God's face was hidden and He 'was troubled', these lines were prophetic. He saw joy 'in the morning'. Only He could ask as in v. 9:
What profit is there in my blood, when I go to the pit?
We have no hint in the Gospels of what took place in the mind of Jesus between His last cry commending His spirit to God's keeping and the Easter Morning question of 'Why weepest thou?' We have however entered into some of the most awful and sacred moments through the reading of such psalms as the 17th, 22nd, and 24th. With reverence let us contemplate Psalm 30 in the setting of His experience of death and the resurrection of His body. It is conceivable that His prayer of praise and thanksgiving to God for the answer to His last cry rose from His spirit even before He took up the body again.

I will extol Thee, O Lord, for Thou has lifted me up
And hast not made my foes to rejoice over me.
O Lord my God, I cried unto Thee and Thou
    hast healed me.
Thou hast brought up my soul from the grave. (v. 1-3)

Here Dr Kay's translation throws more light:

Thou, O Lord, broughtest my soul up from Hades,
Thou savest me alive from among them that go down to
    the pit. (The Psalms translated from the Hebrew. 1871).

This is most dramatic in its literalness. Though David could say this metaphorically, the resurrected Christ (Acts 2:24) could say it thrillingly as a statement of real experience.

He is exultant with song and praises at the victory effected by God. It had been an act of faith on Jesus' part to commend His Spirit to the keeping of the Father; 'whom *God raised* from the dead', say both Peter and Paul. Not that He had doubted or feared, but while He was Man on earth, He must needs exercise the same quality of faith that is given us to enjoy. Now He exults:

Sing unto the Lord, O ye saints of His,
And give thanks at the remembrance of His holiness.

Wonderingly we may ask: Were 'O ye saints of His' those that rose 'and were seen of many'? Or perhaps this address is directed to those trophies of His grace who, liberated from the chains of death, rose with Him and entered in His glorious train when He presented Himself to the Father. The Captain of our salvation, full of manly vigour in His human frame, on rising from the dead, was clothed upon with His Godhead again; and if in the shadow of death He sang, now His thanksgiving resounds with the joy of the stupendous victory accorded by the Father. The shame and horror of darkness are past, and eternal joy is His as He thinks of the glorious outcome —

For His anger endureth but a moment; in His

favour is life:
Weeping may endure for a night, but joy cometh
  in the morning.

And what joy! What a morning!

The words of v. 6, 'In my prosperity I said, I shall never be moved', seem to imply that the speaker's 'prosperity' had been temporarily 'moved'. Jesus had never been without the Father's Presence and He did not perhaps contemplate ever losing it. So much the greater was the blow at its withdrawal.

Now, triumphantly standing on the far side of the grave, alive for evermore, He nevertheless can recall the details of His experience:

Thou didst hide Thy face, and I was troubled.
I cried to Thee, O Lord, and unto the Lord I
  made supplication.

The change here from the vocative second person, 'Thee, O Lord' to the third person, 'unto the Lord', foreshadows the moment when Jesus addressed His Father as My God.

The 'supplication' He mentions now follows: (v. 9,10) —

What profit is there in my blood, in my going down
  into the pit?
Shall the dust praise Thee? Shall it declare the truth?
Hear, O Lord, and have mercy upon me: Lord, be
  Thou my helper.

This petition answered, He now stands, radiant with life and joy, having won life eternal for those who believe.

Hail Redemption's happy morn!

Thou hast turned for me my mourning into dancing:
Thou hast put off my sackcloth and girded me
  with gladness.

If there never was sorrow like unto His sorrow, there was never joy like unto His joy when His mission was done. As another Psalm (45:7) puts it: He was anointed 'with the oil

118

of gladness'. The very lines dance in His thanksgiving. A Welsh poet gives it:

> Thou hast turned my mourning into morning!

But we must look at v. 9 — 'What profit is there in my blood, when I go down to the pit?'

If this is the Redeemer speaking, it is one of the most staggering revelations in the whole of the Psalms. Hades could not hold the King of Life. He had prayed the Father to be the Guardian of His Spirit as He left His Body behind, fixed by the nails to the Cross. Now He has returned from the realms of Death —

> Thou broughtest my soul up from Hades, Thou savedst me alive —

He adds the petition for the sake of the witness to men, that His body may also be raised, for, 'What profit', He argues, 'is there in my blood (if Thou raise not up my body?) Shall the dust praise Thee? Shall it declare the truth? — the truth of physical resurrection? His blood spilt on the dust of Calvary's hill would be only half the story. Men can only know what they see on earth, and of Him only what they saw of His corporal existence. The dust cannot tell the whole truth, He seems to say; hence, let My body rise again, I pray, that men may have proof and believe. (His body would not of course have remained in the tomb. It would have been equally alive had it been invisible to men). 'This commandment have I received of my Father', He said when speaking of His resurrection. ('I have power to take it up again'. John 10:18). He may have asked it.

If there seems to be some contradition between this prayer for His physical resurrection and His own words foretelling it, a profound truth begins to unfold. It is that although Jesus had the power in Himself to rise again, His accustomed deference to the Father caused Him to request it as His gift.

There is something profoundly sacred in the thought that He left His blood spilt on the dust of this earth when He went 'down into the pit'. He did not need it there. It had served its purpose surging healthily in His veins while He talked to men, and then it was poured out generously for men upon the altar of God's wrath. He went 'down to the pit' not as a human being but as the Spirit of Almighty God. The Blood remained on the ground, its witness henceforth ineffaceable, forever proclaiming the extent of God's love and His desire to save. As the poet says, from the dust there blossoms red, LIFE that shall endless be!

The Psalm concludes with the thanksgiving for His resurrection because it brings glory to God:

> Thou hast put off my sackcloth and girded me
> with gladness:
> *To the end that* my soul may sing praise to Thee . . .
> O Lord my God, I will give Thee thanks for ever.

If the title is correctly placed at the head of this psalm, in the context of the series the inferenoe is the dedication of the glorified tabernacle or 'house', His resurrection body, which the Son will retain throughout eternity.

PSALM 31.

It is in this Psalm that there occurs, almost unexpectedly, the sublime yet portentous last word of the crucified Christ. Verse 5:

> Into Thy hands I commit my spirit.

Let us consider the whole psalm with this in view and reverently ask if we have here in human words written the private thoughts of the Saviour as the last moments arrived. There can be no doubt that Psalm 22 is not only prophetic but was actually in the mind of the Redeemer as He bore the world's sins on the Tree. The 29th Psalm offered a glimpse into what possibly were His grateful thoughts as He returned from the 'pit' of Hades. Perhaps the present psalm may be found to fall into place somewhere between the two, on the borderland, one side or the other, of death.

With Psalm 31, by taking v. 5 as our cue, we continue with the utmost reverence to contemplate what thoughts went on within, while that eloquent and austere Figure hung silently between heaven and earth, paying the penalty for man, bridging the gap between God and ourselves, winning our redemption.

It begins:

> In Thee, O Lord, do I put my trust:
> . . . deliver me in Thy righteousness.

Before settling the account with the last drops of His human acquired blood, He prepares to deal the death blow to His enemy Satan. He will not go in His own strength, even He.

> Bow down Thine ear to me; deliver me speedily:
> Be Thou my strong rock, for an house of defence
>   to save
> For Thou art my rock and my fortress;
> Therefore, for Thy name's sake lead me and
>   guide me.
> Pull me out of the net that they have laid privily
>   for me.
> For Thou art my strength.

These petitions are not the unhappy cries of one who fears death but a prayer of conscious dependence on God coupled with profound confidence that He is at hand to save, as we gather from the words that follow now; Into Thine hand I commit my spirit. (v. 5). As at the tomb of Lazarus He was able to say: I thank Thee that Thou hast heard me, and I knew that Thou hearest me always', so now He is both heard and immediately answered.

How profoundly revealing is the prayer of v. 4 in this context, for we learn that even Christ felt it right and necessary to ask strength of God and to request that He be freed from the "net" or trap of death, though He had life in Himself. His prayer also for direction and guidance as He enters the shades shows His entire dependence upon God. On committing Himself to the care of the Father, He receives the assurance He asks, for He adds:

Thou hast redeemed me, O God of truth.

What a wonderful title in the mouth of the trusting Son for the faithful Father! He stakes all on God's fidelity to His promise.

The psalm continues, verses 6-8:

I have hated them that regard lying vanities:
　　but I trust in the Lord.
I will be glad and rejoice in Thy mercy:
　　for Thou hast considered my trouble . . .
And hast not shut me up into the hand of the enemy:
Thou hast set my feet in a large room.

The victory is seized by faith. As when Joshua went forward on the strength of God's promise that 'every place that the sole of your foot shall tread upon, that have I given unto you'. (Josh. 1:3), so Jesus (in this psalm), about to tread down very Hell and assert His dominion over Satan's last redoubt, is confident that victory shall be His, for, by His resurrection He will be able to say, 'Thou hast set my feet in a large room' (place). He was not 'shut up into the hand of the enemy'.

Meanwhile His last physical strength is draining away. His sufferings are very great (vs. 9-13):

Have mercy on me, O Lord, for I am in trouble;
Mine eye is consumed with grief, and my bones
　　with sighing;
My strength faileth because of my misery, and
　　my bones are consumed.

It is not possible to associate the word 'iniquity' with the Saviour's person. Although 'He was *made sin* for us' and thus identified Himself with the sins that were laid upon Him, this explanation seems to be out of place here because of its position in the psalm *after* 'Into Thy hand . . .' Therefore the R.S.V. translation of 'my misery' seems more appropriate, and truly His misery was great as He hung there;

> ... My bones are consumed, I was a reproach
>   among all mine enemies
> But especially among my neighbours ...

He has become 'a fear to my acquaintance'. It was dangerous to be known as His follower, as Peter found out, and the Gospels confirm that 'when they saw me they fled from me'. (v. 11). The pathetic catalogue continues:

> I am forgotten as a dead man out of mind:
> I am like a broken vessel.
> for I have heard the slander of many ...
> ... they took counsel together against me;
> They devised to take away my life.

The fact that these poignant statements are in the first person (as in Psalms 26 and 30) gives a keener edge to the words, since they obviously express the Saviour's own sufferings. The Pharisees His enemies had met together against Him, His good was evil spoken of in slander, His personal friends had fled; He is now like a broken vessel, cast aside, alone. This was all too clearly the human aspect of the crucified Jesus to those who had gathered to see Him die. Every item is ratified by the Gospel narrative.

'A broken vessel'. This was true of His outward appearance. The beauty and perfection of the true portrait was hidden, to be revealed only to those who loved Him, afterwards. The beloved disciple says on several occasions: He was in the world, ... and the world knew Him not ... When therefore He was risen from the dead, His disciples remembered that He had said this unto them; and they believed the scripture and the words which Jesus had said. (John 1:5,10,14; 2:17,22; etc.) He Himself declared that 'the Scriptures ... testify of me'. (John 5:39) and added, 'It is written in the prophets, And they shall be all taught of God'. (6:49). It is therefore only by the illumination of the Holy Spirit that it is given to men to discern His true Person and recognize in Him the Lord of glory who died in ignominy (tremendous paradox!) that He might raise us with Himself to glory!

He prays silently now for vindication and God's favour in the final issue —

> But I trusted in Thee, O Lord;
> I said, Thou art my God, my times are in Thy hand:
> Deliver me from the hand of mine enemies,
> And from them that persecute me.

He had not been 'delivered' from His human enemies. They had been God's instruments to bring about the work of Redemption, and deliverance was not possible. But He is praying for deliverance from the powers of Death and Hell. He continues:

> Make Thy face to shine upon Thy servant,
> Save me for Thy mercies' sake —

and asks that lying lips be put to silence. His request is:

> Let me not be ashamed, O Lord; for I have called
> upon Thee.

He is praying for the final victory which He knows will be achieved by the power of God, and when His resurrection gives irrefutable proof that all He claimed was true, then verily the lying lips (v. 18) will be for ever put to silence and the grievous slander refuted.

How touching is the request of v. 14, couched in the words of the formal High Priestly blessing (Numbers 6). He asks God's blessing before assaying the dreadful task. It is with the peace of God's Presence shining upon His Servant that the heart of the Redeemer now rises in praise and thanksgiving:

> O how great is Thy goodness,
> Which Thou hast laid up for them that fear Thee,
> Which Thou hast wrought for them that trust in Thee
> Before the sons of men!
> Thou shalt hide me in Thy presence . . .
> Blessed be the Lord: for He hath shewed me
> His marvellous kindness in a strong city.

Was this 'strong city' the stronghold of Satan which He is about to invade? He used a like metaphor Himself, speaking of His power to cast out devils: How can one enter into a strong man's house and spoil his goods except he first bind the strong man? and then he will spoil his house. (Matt. 12:29). Recalling His terrible desolation, He continues:

> For I said in my heart, I am cut off from
> before Thine eyes:
> Nevertheless Thou heardest the voice of my
> supplications . . .

With the closing words of this Psalm He as it were girds Himself for His final battle. He is already entering those shadows, for He admonishes the 'saints' to love the Lord, for 'the Lord preserveth the faithful'. These may be the ones who, having died in faith, were awaiting their Liberator. He speaks words of encouragement as He comes to their rescue:

> Be of good courage, and He shall strengthen your heart,
> All ye that hope in the Lord.

The words were equally applicable to His own heart as when God encouraged Joshua — 'Have not I commanded thee? Be strong and of a good courage; . . . for the Lord thy God is with thee'. (Josh. 1:9). With this cry of encouragement, therefore, to those awaiting His salvation, He girds Himself for the great assault.

PSALM 32.

The series opens with 'Blessed is he . . .', 'blessed is the man'. This seems to give the clue to the understanding of the whole, especially if we compare it with the only other psalm so to start, the First Psalm, thus identifying the Speaker of the whole series. That He is the Righteous Man, the Messiah, the Suffering Servant, we have evidence in verses 3 and 4. But this Righteous Man is different. The psalm is retrospective. The writer has a new outlook and new cause for praise. In Himself the Central Character has not changed. He is still the same Person, as the rest of the Psalm shows, but now God is His hiding-place, His refuge, as well as His Instructor, His Guide; He calls upon all the righteous to be glad in Him and rejoice. The difference is that He — the Upright, Sinless, Pure-hearted Just One who had never walked in the way of sinners, now knows how blessed it is that transgressions are forgiven.

This is no contradiction. We stand in awe and amazement, with sorrow and reverence, to realize that the name given to Him by John the Baptist is literally true. He was 'the Lamb of God which taketh away the sin of the world'. There is a new chastened tone, the note of humble gratitude of 'the man unto whom the Lord imputeth not iniquity' (v. 2) after having (v. 5) 'acknowledged my sin unto Thee . . . : I said, I will confess my transgressions unto the Lord, and Thou forgavest the iniquity of my sins. Selah.' What sin? What transgressions? The awed silence of the Selah tells of those that were laid on Him and which He bore and confessed as though they had been His own; and they were forgiven, because the Blood had been shed in ransom.

This was the cause of His great joy, because He knew that 'having offered one sacrifice for sins for ever' (Heb. 10:12) He had obtained eternal redemption for us. (Heb. 9:12). Hence the closing injunction of the Psalm:

Be glad in the Lord, and rejoice, ye righteous,
And shout for joy all ye that are upright in heart,

for God now imputeth not iniquity unto you and in His sight ye are righteous and upright, because your transgressions are forgiven.

A careful comparison of this 32nd psalm with the previous one shows parallels of thought and even some phrases in common. That they are so similar is a help in placing it within the experience of Jesus. Verse 5 of Psalm 31 puts it immediately before the dismissal of His Spirit, and concludes with the address of encouragement to 'all ye His saints' (31:23), the parallel here being that to 'ye righteous' and 'all ye that are upright in heart'. (32:11).

By following this clue, the central portion of both psalms is also found to contain similarities, such as 31:7 —

> I will be glad and rejoice in Thy mercy,

and 32:11 —

> Be glad in the Lord and rejoice . . .

v. 10 —

> Mercy shall compass him about.

His physical and moral sufferings are important in both;

Mine eye is consumed with grief, . . .
My life is spent with grief and my years with
      sighing. (v. 9)
My strength faileth . . . my bones are consumed . . .
I am like a broken vessel. (vs. 10,12).

And in Psalm 32:3 —

> My bones are waxed old, . . .
> Day and night Thy hand was heavy upon me;
> My moisture is turned into drought of summer.

But the new element is that of rogation for pardon, and the blessedness of knowing forgiveness, while in the former psalm the emphasis is on the committal to God while the atonement is being made (vs. 5,17), and faith that the sacrifice will be accepted.

Further there is the parallel of 31:20 —

> Thou shalt hide them in the secret of Thy presence . . .
>   secretly in a pavilion,

and 32:7,

Thou art my hiding-place . . .
Thou shalt compass me about . . .

The first is about others, the second present, is personal, and forgiveness has been vouchsafed.

Where and what is the 'hiding-place', the 'pavilion' of refuge? It is, in the Lord's own words, 'As Thou, Father, in me, and I in Thee'. (John 17:21).

This psalm being in dialogue form, the variety of the personal pronouns serves to identify the various speakers:

v. 1   'he . . . the man . . . whose transgression is
          forgiven . . .'
v. 3   'I kept silence . . .; Thy hand was heavy upon
          me . . .' v. 7.
v. 5   'I acknowledge my sins . . .;'

The speaker in v. 5 is the same as that of v. 3 and 4: the One on whom God's hand was heavy (v. 4) is the One who (v. 5) confessed transgression and received God's forgiveness, as did the High Priest for the people. Hence the 'he' of v. 1 is Himself, but also, any man whose transgression is forgiven, because He has made forgiveness possible. (Heb. 2:17). It behoved Him to be made like unto his brethren. He identified Himself with man as far as it was possible to do so; without sin Himself, but made sin for us.

Further pronouns:

v. 6   For this shall everyone that is godly pray
          unto thee . . .

v. 7   Thou (three times) addressed to God by the first
          speaker.

v. 8   I . . . — is not the 'I' of vs. 3 and 5. It is God
          speaking to His Servant: He will teach Him and
          guide Him. The Servant is dependent on God for
          this; it is an untrodden path.

The advice in v. 9 seems odd in this context. Who are 'ye'? — Be ye not as the horse or as the mule.

If the former psalm, 31, be ascribed to the Christ at the

moment of the committal of His Spirit to God's keeping, this one (32) by comparison contains matter which would indicate the very threshold of the descent to Sheol, the place of Death, where God will compass Him about and has promised to instruct and guide Him. Perhaps therefore v. 9 may be the address to the spirits imprisoned there (I Pet. 3:19). Those who had died in faith 'saw light', they are the 'upright' (34:5;36:9) but the others were counselled against pride and rebellion. Messiah proclaims to them the mercy now available:

> He that trusteth in the Lord, mercy shall compass
> him about. (v. 10).

This is the message that the Saviour preached there. Those that had died before were offered the same salvation, that is, that on acceptance of Him as their Redeemer, by faith they are justified and their sins forgiven (see I Pet. 4:6). Their obedience is then required, their duty being to rejoice and to testify together with all the righteous, among whom they are now counted. (cf. Ephes. 2.)

> Be glad in the Lord, and rejoice, ye righteous:
> And shout for joy, all ye that are upright in heart.

Heavenly beings rejoiced when He was sent and became Man; the Lord Jesus rejoiced that He had given satisfaction to the Father by bringing salvation to men, and the redeemed souls are now invited, nay, commanded to share in the holy joy of God. The very next psalm is the glad anthem of praise as the voices of men join the heavenly music with 'a new song'.

One thinks of the double challenge in Psalm 24 — Was the reiterated question, Who is the King of Glory? merely a dramatic device? Though this may be so, it seems likely that there were two enterings, the first when Christ presented Himself to the Father (after Mary saw Him in the garden and before He appeared to the Twelve); and the second at the Ascension. We do not know if the firstfruits of His labours accompanied Him at the first entry or the second. According to the Gospel narrative, the saints came out of their graves at His resurrection, went into the holy city and appeared unto many. (Matt. 27:53), which could have been in appearances as brief as that of Christ to Mary, or lasting forty days until the Ascension. As the High Priest, Jesus presented the firstfruits to God, Himself being the firstborn of many to follow. (I Cor. 15:20).

Finally, it is illuminating to read chapters 14 to 17 of John's Gospel here, for the instructions inferred by this Psalm to have been spoken by the Redeemer to the believing souls in Sheol, are very like those that Jesus gave before His death to His disciples, i.e., Serve with love, use the refuge or hiding-place that I have provided, and, Be glad, testify and rejoice. Besides, the prayer in John 17 is as apt to be spoken on the accomplishing of the Redemption as when He prayed for His disciples: I have finished the work Thou hast given me to do . . . I have manifested Thy name . . . I have given them Thy word . . . Keep them from the evil — (Hide them in Thy secret pavilion. Psalm 31 and 32). The parallel with His discourse to the disciples is near enough to claim that the instruction in the psalm is equally applicable to either audience.

Summing up: This psalm continues in the setting and furthers the 'teaching' of Psalm 31. The assurance to the redeemed, whether spirits or His human contemporaries, and to us now is: Because I live, ye shall live also. (John 14:19). Therefore, Praise, and shout for joy.

PSALM 33.

This is the psalm that contains the injunction to 'Sing a new song' (v. 3). This coincides with the sequence of thought that links the psalms of this group, the Act of Redemption. The outcome of the Lamb's victory is the universal outburst into a 'new song', the Song of the Redeemed: praise to God for His faithfulness, v. 4; righteousness, goodness, v. 5; power, v. 6; mercy, v. 18; salvation, v. 19; holiness, help and defence (vs. 20,21). The list of attributes is comparable with those addressed to the

Lamb in Revelation ch. 5, Who is 'worthy to receive power, riches, wisdom, strength, honour, glory and blessing'. Each of the attributes named in the Psalm as qualities displayed by God toward man are to be found in the character and behaviour of Christ as portrayed by John. The 'new song' of the psalm (v. 3) is for the souls of the faithful, the 'righteous' of v. 1, who entered with Christ into glory at His Resurrection. They sing praises unto God at once and need not wait until the multitude offer praise to the Lamb. But the New Song of Revelation 5 will still be truly 'new' to all because they no longer have to 'wait', 'hope', or ask for mercy. Their salvation is complete. All, 'they' and 'we' (v.11) are together 'made perfect'. (Heb. 11:39). Paul makes this clear: '. . . the holy Spirit of promise which is the earnest of our inheritance until the redemption of the purchased possession, unto the praise of His glory.' (Eph. 1:13,14). We are 'quickened together with Christ' (Eph. 2;4-6), but not until the final great consummation of all things shall we in the resurrection body know the fullness of His grace, being 'the spirits of just men made perfect'. (Heb. 12:23).

PSALM 34.

This psalm, coming as it does, right in the midst of the Calvary scene, is the more striking as a psalm of faith and hope. It has overtones of an address to a group or congregation, mingled with a personal testimony of God's goodness to the speaker in a recent experience of his own. He invites them —

> O magnify the Lord with me, and let us exalt
> His name together.

And he witnesses to the Lord's dealings with himself —

> I sought the Lord, and He heard me,
> and delivered me from all my fears.

Then comes, interposed, a descriptive comment —

> They looked unto him, and were lightened,
>   and their faces were not ashamed —
>   (or, 'grew radiant').

The personal witness continues —

> This poor man cried, and the Lord heard him
>   and saved him out of all his troubles.

Although this statement can be grammatically interpreted as the testimony of the speaker making the invitation, it also evokes the poignant picture of the repentant thief, the 'poor man' whose soul had 'this day' joined the 'saints' whom the Lord had heard and saved.

From v. 7 onward, one hears an account of the Saviour's address to the waiting spirits. They are assured of God's loving care —

> The angel of the Lord encampeth round about
>   them that fear Him and delivereth them.

One thinks of the verse in Psalm 139 —

> Whither shall I go from Thy spirit? or whither
>   shall I flee from Thy presence?
> If I ascend up into heaven, Thou art there:
> If I make my bed in Hell, behold Thou!

The address continues —

> O taste and see that the Lord is good . . .
> O fear the Lord, ye His saints . . . (v 9).

He invites them to draw near and listen —

> Come, ye children, hearken unto me:
> I will teach you the fear of the Lord. (v. 11).

His instructions follow:

Do good, seek peace, and pursue it . . . (v. 14).

There follow words of encouragement and comfort:

> The eyes of the Lord are upon the righteous
> and his ears are open to their cry. (v. 15).
> . . . The righteous cry and the Lord heareth and
> delivereth
> The Lord is nigh unto them that are of a broken heart.

The statement that 'He keepeth all his bones, not one of them is broken' (present, v. 20), would indicate the hour when Jesus' body hung lifeless, His soul having departed, not yet back to the Father but to Sheol. By contrast the bones of the two thieves have been broken.

What we have gathered from the former psalms of this series leads us to understand that 'they' in v. 5 and 'ye children' v. 11, refers to those in Sheol who, having died in the faith of God, beheld their Deliverer, bringing light and life into the place of Death. Did they gather round Him there with their prayer for salvation? 'God heareth the righteous'. His gracious reply is:

> The Lord redeemeth the soul of His servants.

Note the plural, and compare with 'This poor man' and the 'I' of the Speaker, who leads the praises to God for the deliverance, for —

> None of them that trusted in Him shall be desolate.

He is there, among them. They are invited to join Him in the Song of Praise. They are now the "children" whom God 'having predestinated unto the adoption of children by Jesus Christ to Himself . . . to the praise of the glory of His grace, wherein He hath made us accepted in the Beloved, in whom we have redemption through His blood, the forgiveness of sins . . . that in the fulness of time He might gather in one all things in Christ . . . that we should be to the praise of His glory. (Ephes. 1:5-12).
They thus form the 'congregation' referred to in Psalms

22:15; 35:18; and 40:9,10, to whom He would 'declare Thy name' — the name of Jehovah in its meaning of SAVIOUR.

☆   ☆   ☆

PSALM 35.

Summary: v. 1-3 Appeal to the Lord God to 'plead my cause' and 'stand up for my help'. Note the vocabulary of the warrior: fight, shield, buckler, spear.

    v. 4-8 Imprecations against those who 'seek after my soul' and 'devise my hurt', not the 'wicked' in general but those that persecute Him personally.

    v. 4-6 Vocabulary descriptive of Sheol: confusion, chase, way dark and slippery, persecute, pursue, net in a pit, net laid, pit digged, catch, fall, destruction.

    v. 9-10 Effect of the appeal — My soul shall be joyful . . ., shall praise . . .

    v. 11-16 Recalls recent behaviour of His persecutors. Describes persecution: false witnesses, laid things to my charge, rewarded me evil for good, took spoil of my soul; tore me, gnashed at me with their teeth; mockers . . .

    vs. 13,14 contrasts His own behaviour: He is sympathetic, tender, compassionate, loving.

    vs. 17,18 Challenge and petition to God. Note phrases of Psalm 22:20,21 — 'given my darling to the lions'; I will give thanks in the great congregation', etc.

    vs. 19-27 Appeal to God for His intervention.

    v. 28 Final verses: Vow, or anticipation: He will witness publicly and offer praise continually when His prayer is answered.

It is discovered that, in the present circumstances of this

psalm (in Sheol, prophetically of Christ's experiences there),

a. He feels the need of God's help. v. 1, 3, 10, 17, 22.
b. Though He came to save, He passes judgment on those who reject His salvation and have sought to destroy Him.
c. He states that the victory will come through God's help and cause praise and honour to be given, not to Himself but to God. vs. 18, 25, 27. The victory was to be to the glory of the Father, as He said, cf. John 5:30; 6:38; 7:18; 12:28.

This is exactly the attitude held by Jesus on earth, as He Himself describes it. The same is true of the believer's life today. We have been saved 'to praise the glory of His grace, wherein He hath made us accepted in the Beloved, that we should be to the praise of His glory.'

Since the main purpose of the present exploration of the Psalms is to trace therein possible parallels with the experiences of Jesus Christ as shown in the Gospels, with the aim of learning something of the working of His mind and His character, let us pause here to summarize:

The Character of the Speaker in Psalms 31 to 35.

The thread that runs through all these psalms and binds them together is the spirit of trust based on a personal knowledge of the One trusted. The speaker habitually refers to or addresses God with the deference owed to a superior as would an emissary to his highest authority, but with such natural confidence and ease that relationship is shown to be nearer and more personal, more like that of son to father, although these terms are never used. The intimacy and unity of spirit evinced bespeaks a state of uninterrupted communion between them, to the degree that a single will is seen to activate or motivate both, sufficient to justify the statement that it is the same Person, one being the Human

Counterpart of the Other.

The human composer of these psalms was David, but it is evident that their significance transcends the limitations of man. Let us attribute them to Christ and learn something further about His character from this group of psalms.

The Speaker submits to great physical suffering and plumbs the depths of anguish, but above and through it all there shines a rainbow of praise illumined by faith. His absolute confidence in the One to Whom He prays produces spontaneous exclamations of trust and devotion. A strong determination to accept all as permitted and indeed ordained for Him by the Higher Will, sustains Him. He finds joy in fulfilling that will and bursts into praise and thanksgiving even in the midst of sorrow, not necessarily because relieved from the suffering, for often the exclamations of grief and complaint continue later, but because the soul is renewed by contact with its source, God, as though almost literally it had received a draught from that River of God which had figured so prominently in His meditations. Here in its very unfolding is discerned the pattern described by Paul: 'the mind that was in Christ Jesus . . . who being in the form of God, thought it not robbery to be equal with God: but . . . took upon him the form of . . . man; he humbled himself and became obedient unto death . . .'. (Phil. 2:3-8).

His moral strength is manifest in perseverance and patience. His submission and meekness denote a mind not weak but powerfully exerted to control a natural reluctance to bear ignominy and persecution.

His strength is also revealed in the quality of His courage and endurance. Aware of the antagonism around Him and of probable further victimization, He still remains faithful to His assignment, His vision fixed on the glorious outcome. Strong as is His spirit, however, He does not proceed in His own strength, nor is He coldly stoic. He prays for help — 'Pull me out of the net' (31) — and God promises to lead and guide Him. (32:8). Although His cries are sometimes exceedingly urgent, He is confident that His prayer will be heard: 'I trusted in the Lord.'

His soul's sublime trust does not make Him immune to the effects of persecution. Through autobiographical descriptions we learn what depths of suffering He plumbed, such as the sense of mortal weakness and weariness, the sorrow of human solitude, 'forgotten as a dead man out of mind' (31). He feels 'cut off'. In such terms He prays for the light of God's countenance to shine upon Him and either patiently waits, prayerfully expectant, or, laying hold by faith on future deliverance, exclaims at God's goodness and mercy.

What wounds Him most keenly is slander, but in spite of all He knows the comfort of a secret hiding place for His soul. His inner being is hidden in the 'pavilion' of God's Presence, or as it seems more often, His Spirit being One with God, He dwells in that Presence on high even when corporally He is on earth, vulnerable to physical sorrow and pain. He later calls on others to share the human experience to love and trust the Lord and walk in His will, thus they will receive strength in the process, as He has. His instruction is not cold dogma: it is His harvest from personal experience. 'Hope in the Lord', He says, 'for He preserveth the faithful'. His teaching palpitates with the warmth of conviction, of faith tried in the fire. Cf. I Pet. 1:7. "That the trial of your faith, being much more precious than of gold . . . though it be tried with fire, might be found unto praise and honour and glory . . ."

In some of these psalms He is seen in the very act of undergoing the experience; in others He looks back on it as recent, and describes it to the glory of God, that others may learn of God's tender mercies, His loving-kindness, and His power to save. His joy is to instruct others with the teaching He has received from God while being put to the test. This reveals a generosity of spirit embracing all men. He will gladly tell them of this secret source of Strength, and joyfully encourages them to try the same for themselves. His greatest happiness is in the fact that by doing so — getting others also to trust — He will be the means of bringing still greater glory to God. He will 'cause the upright to shout for joy'. (32).

His heart continually rises in joyful praise while He enjoins men to do the same: Sing a new song! I have proved to you that the word of the Lord is true! Your trust will in due time be justified by God's faithfulness. So, hope in the Lord and rest. In His exuberance He sees all nature as testifying to God's power and goodness (33). He rejoices that He has great cause to extol and magnify the name of the Lord; His soul makes its boast in the Lord (34) proclaiming that God is faithful. But His words are not a mere pious recitation of an aphorism. He is joyfully publishing an experience and brings His own testimony to bear. In brief this is: 'I sought the Lord and He heard me, and delivered me from all my fears'. (34). Let men not shrink from painful trials and testing. He can assure them that 'the Lord is nigh unto them of a broken heart and saveth such as be of contrite spirit'. (34:18). None who trust Him shall be desolate. (v. 22).

This Person, the Speaker of these psalms, is not vindictive but He calls upon God to witness the hurt inflicted upon Him and His adversaries, or affirms His own blamelessness. He is sensitive to men's moral cruelty and their insidiousness. 'They rejoice at my adversity, but when they were sick I fasted. The abjects gathered together against me, and I knew it not.' (35). He calls upon God to bestir Himself — 'How long wilt Thou look on?' Yet with it all He sees Himself returning thanks and praising God 'in the great congregation' of the righteous redeemed. His faith and His hope are unmoved, and like Michael the Archangel when contending with the devil for the body of Moses, He leaves it to God to rebuke His enemies. (Jude 9). He vows eternal praise: 'My tongue shall speak of Thy righteousness and of Thy praise all the day long' — and there is no night there!

Here, then, we have the inner workings of the mind of the Sent One, the Kinsman Redeemer, the Man Christ Jesus, God in human form, the Link between God and man, who can of His own nature commune directly and intimately with God yet who at the same time was 'touched with the feeling of our infirmities'. In these psalms He approaches the Holiest in His own right; He is able to stand up confidently and offer to be judged by the righteous God (35:24) though He is in the flesh as it were, with His feet veritably on earth: 'and let them (his enemies) not rejoice over me'. His real humanity is seen in the Gospels, needing food and drink, rest and sleep, shown to be capable of thirst and weariness and of shedding tears. Here He is shown experiencing the whole gamut of human emotions to its depth yet living on spiritual heights which prove Him to be the Same Who inhabited the regions of light. God took upon Himself a human frame vulnerable to persecution and even (temporary) physical death. He suffered as man suffers but was also divine. He knew dread, though not fear. He felt oppression but not defeat, He had to exercise faith and hope in that He had to wait for the deliverance that He believed would come. He was 'sorrowful yet always rejoicing' (II Cor. 6:10). By faith He was certain of final victory and could therefore exult in the Lord and bless all those that favoured His righteous cause by including them in His own vow to magnify the Lord for ever.

The epistles and the story of the early Church show that He set the pattern for His followers and disciples (and ourselves), who delivered us from so great a death, and doth deliver, in whom we trust that He will yet deliver us. (II Cor. 1:10). We are, as He was, 'troubled on every side, yet not distressed; we are perplexed, but not in despair, persecuted, but not forsaken; cast down, but not destroyed ... that the abundant grace might through thanksgiving of many redound to the glory of God ... and though our outward man perish, yet the inward man is renewed day by day'. (II Cor. 4:8,9,15). As dying and behold we live (II Cor. 6:9).

If the Psalms thus far show different facets of the jewel that is Jesus hidden in them, each psalm showing a part of the whole, Psalm 36 suddenly presents in synthesis, and in its complete setting, the great Gem Himself, for the Son is still the central figure. No longer the Sufferer on earth, He is the Second Person of the holy Trinity in His rightful place, (cf Rev. 7:15-17) 'in the midst of the Throne', the Intercessor, Redeemer and Shepherd of the just (the 'children of men' who have 'put their trust in Him'; v. 7,b). This more than panoramic view — this universal context of the Son's service and mission — gives a glimpse of the whole story, from past eternity to endless eternity to come, in a flash.

'Behold I set before you the way of life and the way of

death'. (Jer. 21:8). Psalm 36 does both.

PSALM 36.

This remarkable psalm gives up its secrets only to the persevering inquirer. Opening with a description of the wicked (vs. 1-4), it continues for its greater part with a contrasting picture — not of the Righteous Man but of God Himself (v. 5-10); v. 11 tells of the daily malevolence with which the righteous are harassed; and the final verse (12) briefly states the end of the wicked.

On examining this structure carefully, we find that the opening verses correspond to the triad of evil depicted in the Apocalypse:

v 1. The incitement to rebellion by Satan. There is 'no fear of God before his eyes'.
v. 2. corresponds to the Creature who, claiming to be God 'flatters himself in his own eyes'. (II Thess. 2:4; Rev. 13:2,6,7).
v. 3 to the Antichrist or False Prophet, 'the words of his mouth are iniquity and deceit'. (Rev. 13:14;19;20).
v. 4 is again in three parallel statements which complete the Apocalyptic pattern, the spirits devising evil, seeking evil and doing evil.

On noticing this tripartite structure one is led to examine the second part of the Psalm for the Trinity of Holiness, and there it is:

vs. 5-7 speak of the Father, God the Creator.
vs. 8,9 present the Son, 'water', 'life', 'light'. (John 1:4,9;8:12;12:46;)
vs. 10,11 represent the work of the Holy Spirit, teaching, delivering. It is He that is able to keep us from falling. (Jude 24).

The psalmist prays for the continuance of God's loving-kindness to the upright in heart.

Having found that this presentation of the Holy Trinity does not conclude the Psalm but that there is a further, final reference to the wicked with 'the workers of iniquity

. . . are cast down, and shall not be able to rise', one may wonder what part this verse plays in the structural pattern of the whole, for it would seem that it more properly belongs to the opening section which describes the wicked. Analysis shows that part I (vs. 1-7) tells what takes place on earth; part II (vs. 8-10) has its setting in heaven ('the fatness of Thy house', 'river of Thy pleasures', 'the fountain of life', 'Thy light'). And v. 12, telling where the 'workers of iniquity are, is hell.

But why, one may ask, does such a magnificent picture start with 'the transgression of the wicked' rather than with the description of God's attributes? Perhaps it is because the spiritual history of man's downfall and the need for a plan of redemption starts with Satan's rebellion. The Wicked One and his evil intent existed before man did, and it was his transgression ('no fear of God, iniquity, hate, deceit) which caused God's plan of salvation to be drawn up. The story of God's planning for man started when Lucifer was cast out of his high position in Heaven. Hence the order of the drama set forth in this psalm is correct, and the Creation comes after the transgression (or rebellion) of the Wicked One. One may therefore further claim that this Psalm sets forth in synthesis the whole of the Scriptures in their correct chronological order, as follows:

vs. 1-4   The trangression of the Wicked One; i.e. the rebellion and fall of Lucifer.
vs. 1-6   The Creator.
v. 7   Israel
vs. 8,9   The Redeemer.
vs. 10,11 The Church Era.
v. 12   The Judgment and the consummation of all things. The Kingdom and the power of His Christ are come. Rev. 12:10.

PSALM 37.

In summary this psalm says: Do not be impatient for the

destruction of the wicked because their end is inevitable and will surely come.

After the first 9 verses, which contain counsel to the godly, nearly every mention of evildoers is balanced or parallel with another or others regarding the upright; sometimes these come first, sometimes the others:

v. 9   Evildoers shall be cut off:
         But those that wait upon the Lord shall inherit the earth.

The series that follows begins each parallel with 'the wicked', until v. 18 which starts — The Lord knoweth the ways of the upright . . . contrasted with — But the wicked shall perish.

Again v. 21 starts a parallel with 'the wicked', but v. 23 opens with —

The steps of a good man . . .

and the psalm continues in this strain until the end of v. 28 which closes with —

. . . but the wicked shall be cut off.

Again, the following verse (29) opens a series of promises to the righteous which outnumber the statements about the end of the wicked, with only one mention until v. 34 which ends —

When the wicked are cut off, Thou shalt see it.

which is not primarily a statement about the wicked.

The general summing up of the statements about the wicked (mentioned 12 times, also evildoers, workers of iniquity, transgressors, the enemies of the Lord, the cursed of the Lord) is that they shall be cut off and perish. But the sentiments about the righteous (the just, v. 12; the upright, vs. 18,37; a good man, 23; His saints, 28; the perfect man, 37; the righteous — seven times — in addition to the first 10 verses which are addressed to 'Thou', identified in v. 6

with 'the righteous' by reference to 'thy righteousness') are more various and constitute a veritable catalogue of blessings: shall dwell in the land, verily to be fed (v. 2); He shall give thee the desires of thine heart(4); He shall bring it (i.e. thy trust) to pass (5); bring forth thy righteousness . . . and thy judgment as the noonday (6); inherit the earth (9,11,22,29,34); shall delight themselves in the abundance of peace (11); the Lord upholdeth (him), (17,24); his inheritance shall be forever (18); not to be ashamed, . . . in the days of famine shall be satisfied (19); his steps ordered by the Lord (23,31); never forsaken (25,28,35); preserved forever (28b); his end is peace (37); the righteous have salvation, strength in time of trouble, help, deliverance (39,40), and shall see the overthrow of the wicked. (34).

There are roughly twice as many promises and reassurances to the upright as there are statements (not threats) about the end of the wicked, which suggests that God is twice as ready to bless as to punish!

It is noteworthy that the verbs and the pronouns are in the singular for both 'the wicked' and the just (cf. v 12), after which, from v. 16 (and over-lapping with 'Thou' in vs. 9,11,14) the catalogue of blessings continues in the 3rd person, but not always singular; v.9 *those* that wait upon the Lord; v. 11, the meek; v. 14 such as be of upright conversation; v. 17 the righteous; v. 18,29,39; such as be blessed of Him (23); His saints. These are interspersed with statements about the righteous, a good man (23); the perfect man (37) — in the singular; and vs. 16,21,25,30. We may draw by inference from v. 12 — The wicked plotteth against the just, and gnasheth upon him with his teeth, — that the reference when in the singular is to the Just One, and to His enemy the Wicked One, thus not merely personifying uprightness and wickedness but identifying them as Christ and Satan. Thus we have here, in the first 12 verses references to Christ, who is shown in contrast with the Wicked One who opposes Him, and after that the references in the plural on both sides suggest the disciples or followers of each.

☆   ☆   ☆

143

Now we may develop the thought which has formed the connecting link of these studies: How does this psalm fit in to the probable thoughts or experiences of Christ while on earth?

There is an initial difficulty in the fact that the teachings of the first 8 verses are addressed to the second person, 'thou', and we can hardly imagine Jesus to be in need of the reminder to 'Fret not thyself because of evil doers', or to 'Cease from anger'. These commands continue in vs.27 and 34: Depart from evil and do good; . . . Wait on the Lord, and keep His way; — but here they come in the "plural" sector of the psalm and might be addressed to 'all those who trust in the Lord.'

But if we think of an occasion when Jesus was perturbed because of the evil He saw about Him, it is not difficult to suppose Him to be using the first part of this psalm in soliloquy, encouraging Himself in the Lord. He is not in need of instruction, but knowing it, He could recall the Father's commands for His behaviour in the flesh. Such an occasion of His spirit being perturbed is narrated in Mark 3:5-7 when He entered the synagogue where the man with the withered hand was and the Pharisees 'watched Him, whether He would heal him on the Sabbath day: that they might accuse Him'. They gave no answer to His challenge of 'Is it lawful?' and when He had 'looked round about on them with anger, being grieved at the hardening of their heart, He saith unto the man, Stretch forth thine hand'. The Pharisees then 'went out, and straightway with the Herodians took counsel against Him, how they might destroy Him'. Jesus with His disciplines withdrew then. May He not, at this juncture, have reminded Himself — 'Fret not because of evil doers, trust in the Lord, and (go on doing) good; . . . commit; . . .rest; — and even 'cease from anger', since 'the meek shall inherit the earth'? He later referred to Himself as 'meek and lowly'. (Matt. 11:29).

This very phrase (v. 11 of this psalm) brings strongly to mind the Beatitudes which opened the Sermon on the Mount, and His more private instructions to His followers in Chapters 6 and 7 of Matthew. 'He taught them as one having authority'. In fact this psalm offers a very close parallel with the Lord's personal teaching to His disciples.

The whole group of these psalms (30-40) being associated with the final part of Jesus' life on earth, from the Crucifixion to the Ascension, this psalm might be thought of as His counsel to His disciples and followers on the road to Bethany for the Ascension (Luke 24:50; Matt. 28:19,20). It is evocative of the style, method, and aim of Jesus' teaching as shown in the Sermon on the Mount, the latter addressed to the multitude, this psalm being the purport of His final talk to His committed followers. The Speaker is the same. This view would confirm who are 'the righteous' in the plural.

PSALM 38.

Like Psalm 31, this is an account, almost a catalogue, of the Redeemer's sufferings and agony on the Cross, moral, physical and spiritual.

v. 2   Thine arrows stick fast in me; Thy hand presseth me sore.

v. 3   There is no soundness in my flesh . . .nor any rest in my bones.

v. 5   My wounds stink and are corrupt (festered).

v. 7   My bones are filled with a loathsome (burning) disease . . .

v. 8   I am feeble and sore broken . . .the disquietness (rapid beating) of my heart . . .

v. 10 My heart panteth, my strength faileth me . . .
       The light of mine eyes is gone from me.

The speaker's aversion in the description of the offensiveness of the disease amounts to horror. He bewails the pollution which has invaded flesh and bone alike. The words used suggest the ravages of leprosy, but we know that David never suffered from any such disease. Our only recourse is to interpret this imagery as prophetical of a physical condition foreign to David's own experience, but which he apprehends spiritually. Leprosy in the Scriptures is the figure of sin. Verses 1-10 of this psalm depict the feelings of horror and loathing felt by the holy Lamb of God as He bore the sins of the world in His sinless body on the tree. One of the most moving features (and one which ratifies this thought) is, that the speaker of the psalm recognizes the blow as having come from God — 'Thine arrows', 'Thy hand', 'Thine anger'. He accepts it (cf Psalm 39:9) 'because Thou didst it.' We may therefore place the thoughts of this psalm in that portion of time of all the most sacred, when the Son on the altar of the Cross received the full blow of the Father's hand which was to provide redemption for mankind.

But the question remains whether we should consider the physical details as literal or metaphorical. The holy and sinless Body could not know corruption. Would v. 5 therefore mean that when men's sin was laid upon Him His flesh became vulnerable to natural laws? We may reverently ask: May the wounds in His hands and feet have begun to inflame? Did the cuts and haematomae, the broken skin caused by the scourgings swell out in awful infirmity, as described here? One hesitates to give the answer, but this psalm suggests that they did, or felt as though they did. When the sin was declared forgiven and purged, the body also was made whole again, but for the mark of the wounds, the imprint of the nails by which the prophet affirms that He will be recognized. (Zech. 13:6).

His moral sufferings were equally severe. They are expressed by such words as (v. 1) — Thy *hot* displeasure; (v. 2) Thy hand presseth *sore*; (v. 6) I am bowed down *greatly*; (v. 8) *sore* broken.

That the sins were not the speaker's own becomes evident from this psalm too. He declares them as though they were His, v. 18, but He states that His adversaries (v. 20) render evil for good 'because I follow the good'.

The reference (v. 11) to 'My lovers and friends' deserting Him and His kinsmen standing afar off points unmistakably to the events at the arrest of Jesus, during his trial, and on the Cross. The reference (v. 12) to 'those that seek after my life', who 'lay snares for me', . . . 'speak mischievous things, and imagine deceits all the day long', exactly describes the manner of His persecution at the hands of the religious leaders. And finally the verse following (v. 13) identifies

Him with the meek Sufferer of Isaiah 53 —

> I was as a dumb man that openeth not his mouth . . .
> And in whose mouth are no reproofs.

Verses 15 to the end are expressions of trust. The tone has changed. It is a modulation of the most moving sweetness when we consider that it was *in the midst* of such extreme heartbreak, with the burden of sin, the isolation of pain and the suffering at the stroke of God's hand, that His heart is laid open:

> Lord, all my desire is before Thee (v. 9).

He trusts at the moment of death that His sacrifice be acceptable and sufficient.

For in Thee, Lord, do I hope: thou wilt hear, O Lord my God. (v. 15). The final request, 'Forsake me not, O Lord; O my God, be not far from me' (v. 21 and 22); Make haste to help me, O Lord of my salvation' — are the cry from the heart of the Saviour on the brink of that pit from whence, in Psalm 40, He tells us, 'The Lord heard . . . and brought me up'.

The important thing to notice is that while He was in the great darkness His trust was pinned on the faithfulness of God to raise Him up and award Him the salvation He was purchasing with His life. This is not only deeply moving, but also greatly illuminating, for it teaches and reveals something that could not have been known by the eye-witness accounts of the Gospels, but which the author of the letter to the Hebrews states: He was heard in that He feared. (Heb. 5:7).

This Psalm is used in the Synagogues on the Day of Atonement.

PSALM 39.

Several lines in this psalm suggest its place in the sequence which recommenced with the 38th psalm, of Christ's sufferings on the Cross:

v. 2 I was dumb with silence, I held my peace,
even from good.
v. 7b My hope is in Thee.
v. 9 I was dumb, I opened not my mouth, because Thou
didst it.
v. 10 Remove Thy stroke from me; I am consumed at the
blow of Thine hand.
v. 12 Hear my prayer, O Lord, and give ear unto my cry,
Hold not Thy peace at my tears.

But there are other verses here that seem quite
incompatible with the Saviour's thought at that period:

v. 1 I will take heed to my ways, that I sin not with my
tongue;
I will keep my tongue with a bridle, while the
wicked is before me.

Take also the request in v. 4 —

Lord, make me to know mine end, and the measure of
my days, what it is.

The Lord Jesus knew why He had come into the world,
but it may be that the foreknowledge of 'the measure of my
days' was part of that which He laid aside on becoming
Man. This prayer again is not one likely to have been
offered at the Crucifixion.

Other lines which seem not to be in tone with the period
in the Messiah's life which this series indicates appear to
echo the dreary pessimism of Ecclesiastes (v. 5,6). But these
should be taken within their context:

Verily every man at his best state is altogether vanity,
Surely every man walketh in a vain show;
Surely they are disquieted in vain:
He heapeth up riches and knoweth not who shall
gather them.

These remarks are preceded by prayer (v. 4), but even so,

are unlikely to have entered Jesus' thoughts at the very hour which He spoke of in John 13:1. However, v. 5 may serve as a starting point:

Verily every man *at his best* state is altogether vanity. Selah. Full and perfect manhood ('man at his best state') in the Scriptures is regarded to be reached at the age of thirty. The Levites of Aaron's line started service in the Sanctuary at the age of 30 (cf. Num. 4:23,30; I Chron. 23:3). (Ordinary levitical service started at the age of 25. Num. 8:24). Luke tells us that 'Jesus was about thirty years of age' when He began to teach. Let us examine the psalm from the standpoint of Jesus when He entered His public ministry, and then the resolution with which it opens takes on additional significance.

I will keep my mouth with a bridle while the wicked is before me — as does the request (v. 4) . . . 'that I may know how frail I am'.

As the holy Son grew up from the age of 12 (legal adulthood) to that of 30, we know that He 'grew in wisdom, in stature, and in favour with God and man' (Luke 2:52). His soul had come from the bosom of the Father and was one of and with the Trinity. His thoughts were still, as they had always been, in harmony with the Father's. Like His mother, He might have 'kept these things' in His heart during those unrecorded years, but while outwardly He lived the life of a human, working in and perhaps taking over the carpentry business of Joseph when the latter died, inwardly He had seen through the eyes of God. He experienced life as it is lived on earth, marked by daily toil, surrounded by the hills and wild flowers of the countryside, and in the little narrow streets of a village. At the same time He had beheld men's need and had thought the thoughts of God.

The call then came to abandon the rather limited sphere of His youth and young manhood, leaving behind the simplicity of a village carpenter's life, to assume the mantle of the Prophet and put on the sandals of the Messenger of God. That message of God's redeeming love toward man must be spread far and wide. Only His human feet could carry, and His voice proclaim it. To do this He had laid aside all the prerogatives of Godhead, and must limit

Himself strictly within human dimensions, even to the suppression of godly indignation when occasion should arouse it. 'I said, I will take heed to my ways, that I sin not with my tongue; I will keep my mouth with a bridle while the wicked is before me'. Not that He might 'sin', but that it would transgress the limits of His voluntary abnegation to unleash Divine wrath. It was not only when He was 'like a sheep before the shearers' that he was dumb. He also 'kept His mouth with a bridle' when the wicked were before Him. It is only when the Lamb is on the Throne (Rev. 5:6; 6:5) that judgment and the power to destroy are in His hands (John 5:22; 8:15). On earth He is the Lamb to be sacrificed to save sinners; He is the Messenger of God's mercy and love, and of His longing that all men should repent and be saved. It is the prerogative of God to destroy the wicked. Hence it would be a "transgression" for Jesus as the Saviour to speak any word that would appear to usurp that power; and it would be an obstacle to the fulfilling of His mission. ('Think ye not that I could call twelve legions of angels . . .?'). He must have thought, at times when His message of God's love was taken lightly and Himself reviled, that these wicked men could be undone by a single look or word of His. He therefore prays that He may forbear.

The prayer also of v. 4: 'That I may know how frail I am', may be interpreted in this light as: Grant that I may apprehend human frailty. Being Divine, He had to discipline Himself to accept the limitations of man. In His physical existence He was not in His accustomed environment, dwelling in Eternity, though His thoughts must still have 'roamed the courts of Heaven'. He endured the 'contradiction (gainsaying) of sinners' against Himself because He had determined at the outset to keep his mouth with a bridle. Verse 4, then, may be paraphrased as: He asks God to keep Him mindful that He is a man, subject to the limits of his human status and of His task.

It is natural that He would become acutely sensitive to the brevity of man's life (v. 6) — 'Surely every man walketh in a vain show . . .' How puny and pointless all their goals and their strivings seemed! 'He heapeth up riches and knoweth not who will gather them!' and v. 11, Thou makest his beauty to consume away like a moth'. As He grew to adulthood He would become more acutely conscious, too, of the brevity of time and of man's life span. 'Behold, Thou hast made my days as a handbreath, and mine age is as nothing before Thee'. The 'Selah' which follows is pregnant with significance. He speaks for mankind.

And now, Lord, what wait I for? (v. 7). The request to know how long he shall live is human and yet it is well nigh impossible to imagine it in the mind of Jesus, who as God, must have known the end from the beginning. That is, if we think of Him as having divine omniscience while on earth. But if we consider that on His inhabiting the flesh He accepted a human being's limitations, this request: 'Make me to know ... the measure of my days,' could possibly have come before His public ministry began. Since He knew He had been sent to accomplish the redemption of man by the sacrifice of Himself, He may sometimes in His vigorous young manhood have wondered when He would be free to begin. He had officially reached adulthood at the age of twelve, and stated that He 'must be about my Father's business', but He remained subject to family authority into His 'teens. When He had reached His full physical development in His twenties He must have wondered when He would receive the Father's command to begin the work He had come to do. ('I held my peace ... while I was musing the fire burned' (v. 2,3). Obviously it could not be done in the peaceful home of the carpenter. His twenties ended, He was thirty years of age before His call came and he went out to meet John baptizing in Jordan. May He not have wondered at 29 how much longer He would have to wait? (v. 7) The inference would be that as a man, the knowledge of God's time was in part withheld from Him as it is from us. Then suddenly the time had come, and the waiting was over. He obeyed the call, and He started on the road that led away from the gentle home of Nazareth, to Jordan, to Jerusalem, to Calvary.

Led of the Spirit, He went to Jordan, where John had proclaimed that coming after him was the Lamb of God that taketh away the sin of the world. As He journeyed thither for His baptism He vowed that He would speak no word beyond the dictates of God's will. (v. 1). Later He could claim that 'I speak nothing of myself, but as my

Father taught me . . . I speak to the world those things that I have heard of Him . . . I do always those things that please Him.' (John 8:26-29).

His submission to the Father was total. His demeanour was meek and lowly. This should never be mistaken for weakness of character. We glimpse, on the contrary, how great was the moral strength that kept under control His indignation and anger at the ungodly, for He was bound to restraint by these vows, and kept them . . . 'I was dumb with silence, I held my peace.' (v. 5). While He was vowed to silence He prays that God will 'hold not Thy peace at my tears.' (v. 12)

> . . . for I am a stranger with Thee, and a sojourner
> (pilgrim) as all my fathers were. (v. 12)
> and cf. Psalm 119:19 — I am a stranger in the earth.

In his prayer at the dedication of the offerings for the building of the Temple David utters the same words: Now, therefore, our God, we thank Thee, and give praise to Thy glorious name . . . For we are strangers before Thee, and sojourners as were all our fathers: our days on earth are as a shadow and there is none abiding . . .(I Chron. 29:10-19).

Thus also prayed the Son of David as He dedicated His all an offering to God on the eve of His going forth on His earthly mission, as He had before the foundation of the world. (Psalm 40): (Then said he, Lo, I come to do Thy will, O my God . . . the offering of the body of Jesus Christ. (Heb. 10:5-10). Unlike David, He was offering not material wealth but was dedicating the body in which He was a sojourner for the building of the Temple not made with hands, eternal in the heavens.

David and his people (I Chron. 29:20-22) then 'sacrificed in abundance, and did eat and drink before the Lord on that day with great gladness.' The Son of God who made this prayer of dedication His own, is still waiting for that glorious day of 'great gladness', for He vowed when He gave thanks for the Cup that He would 'not drink henceforth of this fruit of the vine until the day when I drink it new with you in my Father's kingdom.'

Although the first part of the Psalm suits the opening of

His public ministry, the Messianic 'I opened not my mouth' of v. 9 and the 'blow of thine hand' (v. 10) seem better to fit its closing, and we are again at the Crucifixion. His time on earth had gone so quickly, His 'days no more than a handbreadth' (v. 5) as He reviews His life, and now He is interceding for the trangressors with tears (v. 8), and prays to be heard on the ground of His obedience. He was a "sojourner" because on becoming Man He had been absent from His abode.

The psalm now concludes with the further prayer —

O spare me that I may recover strength before I go hence
and be no more — (a man).

Yea, says Paul, though we have known Christ after the flesh, yet now we know Him so no more. (II Cor. 5:16).

☆   ☆   ☆

PSALM 40.

This psalm takes on the nature of a lyrical drama if we read it in the context of Calvary. It produces an effect that is both sublime and profoundly moving. By contemplating it in the light of the experience of Jesus we find that it must take place between His final cry from the Cross and His resurrection. It is told in retrospect, not as in Psalm 22, a dramatic account at the moment of the experience. He has come back from Sheol and from the tomb and He testifies triumphantly to God's saving power:

He brought me up out of an horrible pit, out
of the miry clay,
And set my foot upon a rock, and established
my goings. (v. 2).

This meant victory for Him and is a cause for the greatest joy:

And He hath put a new song in my mouth,
even praise to our God:

153

Many shall see it and fear, and shall trust in
the Lord (v. 3).

The 'new song' is, in synthesis, v. 4 —

Blessed is the man that maketh the Lord his trust.

Praise continues in v. 5 —

Many, O Lord my God, are Thy wonderful works . . .
And Thy thoughts which are to usward: . . .
They are more than can be numbered.

Having Himself risen, He has brought salvation to many.
Verses 6-8 beginning —

Sacrifice and offering Thou didst not desire

tell the scene in Heaven prior to His coming to earth, and
offers a dramatic explanation of why He ever came to be in
the pit from which He has been saved.

Then said I, Lo, I come: in the volume of the book
it is written of me.
I delight to do Thy will, O my God; yea, Thy law
is within my heart.

God had accepted His offer and His voluntary sacrifice.
As a consequence He underwent the experience which He
refers to as 'an horrible pit' in v. 2. Then He gives an
account of what He did while there: He preached
righteousness to the great congregation (v. 9), and 'declared
Thy faithfulness and Thy salvation'; He also proclaimed
God's loving kindness and His truth. The 'great congregation' is perhaps the waiting spirits to whom He preached (I
Pet. 3:19;4:6). There, meanwhile, 'innumerable evils have
compassed me about' and He cried,

Be pleased, O Lord, to deliver me:
O Lord, make haste to help me,

giving as His reason that His resurrection would vindicate

both Himself and God. Those who had died believing and looked for His salvation would 'rejoice and be glad in Thee', for they would rise with Him. Those who had rejected God would be driven backward and remain desolate, (vs. 14,15) — a most graphic description in these circumstances. Finally He recalls His urgent prayer as He entered that world of despair and darkness:

> Thou are my help and my deliverer: Make no
> tarrying, O my God. (v. 17)

We are left in no doubt as to the speediness of the answer. It was given in:

> v. 1 I waited patiently for the Lord, and He inclined unto me, and heard my cry:
> He brought me up also out of an horrible pit, and set my feet upon a rock.
> And hath put a new song in my mouth, even praise to our God.

This psalm is that 'new song', and Jesus gives praise to God for His deliverance and bodily resurrection, renders an account of the mission He has accomplished, endorsing it by a statement of how He came to be commissioned.

PSALM 41.

Jesus Himself, then His apostles, the evangelists, and later Paul, and more emphatically the writer of the Epistle to the Hebrews, claim the shadowing forth of the Messiah in the Psalms. David knew and in faith apprehended that the Messiah must come of his seed. David was 'a man after God's heart', upright and whole-hearted in his love for God. On a spirit so pliable and docile Godward, the Holy Spirit could play as upon an instrument, causing him to express words of import greater than he knew.

The agonies of the burden of sin far outstrip ordinary human remorse, and the deeply moving complaints may well more fitly express what it meant to the Son of God to carry the world's sin. It is true that certain passages, such as that in Psalm 41, which is thought to have been motivated by a recent serious illness of the author, do not appear to correspond with any event in the life of Jesus — 'bed of languishing, . . . make all his bed in sickness, . . . an evil disease, say they, cleaveth fast unto him, . . .', yet though a period of illness may have been the source of David's psalm, it is no less obvious that a meaning of greater scope can be read into certain parts of the same, notably v. 9 —

Yea, mine own familiar friend, in whom I trusted,
Which did eat of my bread, hath lifted his heel against me,

which portrays Judas, according to some interpreters. The 'enemies' also, of whom David complains, who 'hate me, whisper together against me; against me do they devise my hurt' (v. 7), and who 'speak evil of me (saying), When shall he die and his name perish?' and: 'Now that he lieth he shall rise up no more', are very recognizably of the same sort who 'sought to slay Jesus', conspired for His death, and requested the Roman soldiers to seal the tomb. With all this evidence, it is not difficult to consider the 'bed of languishing' as the Cross.

Yet under no circumstances can v. 4 be attributed to the Saviour:

I have sinned against Thee.

Surely it is David the man that emerges, as in Psalm 51, causing a flaw in the image being prophetically limned in his psalms.

However, we have seen in some psalms, notably 38:18 and 40:15, that the Messiah may be heard 'declaring' sins as though they were His own, at the moment on the Cross when He was purchasing man's pardon and bearing the guilt of every sinner. Sometimes the word 'confess' (32:5) is used, with the meaning of 'tell out, enumerate, declare'; and sometimes the word translated 'sin' has rather the meaning of 'weakness, foolishness', or 'misery'. But in this, the 41st psalm, the words are catagoric — unless the original throws

better light on them —

> I said, Lord, be merciful to me:
> Heal my soul, for I have sinned against Thee.

That He should acknowledge for forgiveness the sins of others is one thing, but that He should state that He Himself had sinned is difficult to accept, if not inadmissible. But propelled by the sequence of these psalms and realizing the oneness of the whole, we must admit the conclusion that the bearing of the guilt made Him the sinner in God's eyes. We cannot truly apprehend the dark depths of this truth but how profoundly dreadful it is can be glimpsed through the Messianic application of these psalms.

We have noticed that Psalms 25 to 31 correspond with the events between the Arrest and the departing of Jesus' Spirit from His Body on the Cross. Perhaps they were composed for the ceremonies of the Great Day of Atonement. A number of the psalms that follow the 30th are linked by the same theme, that of a chastened soul which has undergone some severe spiritual experience of darkness and reverential fear from which it has come forth with new vision and is full of praise and thanksgiving to God. A new colouring is common to all these psalms of the Afflicted One (up to Psalm 41): the chastened spirit has discovered a new quality of joy, a heightened sensitiveness born of pain, like the clear brilliance of sunshine on a hilltop still wet after rain. The sign of sorrow are there, but joy has come in the morning. He tells of both.

Commentators think that these psalms must have been written by David during and after a severe illness of which we have no record. But we may object to this surmise by pointing out that Hezekiah's illness is recorded; why should not also David's if it occurred? A high degree of sensitiveness to sin and anguish at the burden of it characterizes this group of psalms. They do not refer to any specific sin but David's sensitiveness to sin became acute after Nathan's 'Thou art the man'. In the Christian's own experience the same holds true. If he falls into sin, at the time not recognizing it as such, his love for the Lord will convict him and the Lord then deals with him in such a way as to make his act become heinous to him, and the memory of it intolerable. The burden grows through an agony of acknowledgement and repentance, after which his chastened soul is a great deal more aware of sin and careful to avoid it; also he values his cleansing more keenly than before.

PSALMS 31-41.

Since verse 5 of the first psalm of this series points to the period of the Lord's Passion, the cries of affliction, confession and thanksgiving may bespeak the inward anguish of the Saviour as He bore our sins on the Cross. They thus help us to obtain some insight into what it meant for the sinless Son of God to bear the burden of guilt that hid the Father's face.

There are enough allusions to the experience of Messiah scattered throughout this group to justify the assumption that Jesus' thoughts might have been couched in these terms during that terrible ordeal. If He is recognized as the object of certain allusions therein, the whole group should be examined for its applicability. Such allusions to Messianic sufferings are:

> He keepth all my bones, not one of them is
>   broken. (34:20.)

> For without cause they have hid for me their net
>   in a pit, which without cause they have
>   digged for my soul. (35:7).

> False witnesses did rise up, they laid to my charge
>   things that I knew not. 35:11.

> They rewarded me evil for good. 35:12.

> They . . .gathered themselves together against me
>   . . . with hypocritical mockers in feasts they
>   gnashed upon me. 35:15,16.

They hate me without cause. 35:19.

They opened their mouths wide against me and
said, Aha, aha. 35:21.
Yea, mine own familiar friend, in whom I trusted,
which did eat of my bread, hath lifted up
his heel against me. 41:9.

Into Thine hand I commit my spirit. 31:5.

Then said I, Lo, I come, in the volume of the
book it is written of me, I delight to do
Thy will, O God; yea, Thy law is within
my heart 40:7; cf. Heb. 10:9.

Much of the terminology of Psalm 35 is strongly
reminiscent of Psalm 22, universally acknowledged as
Messianic. Psalms 38 and 39 also contain strong allusions:
the strongly indentifying phrase of 'he opened not his
mouth' (cf. Isa. 53) in Psalm 38:13 and 39:9 further point to
Messianic suffering.

I was as a dumb man that openeth not his mouth.
38:13.
I was dumb, I opened not my mouth; because
Thou didst it. 39:9.

I was dumb with silence; I held my peace.
(38:11).

All these expressions are Messianic and of the period of the
Crucifixion. There is also His desertion by friends and
kinsmen. (38:11).
Not only the anguish but also the physical sufferings of
the Saviour are depicted in these psalms. The description of
failing strength as He hangs there is so vivid that it may be
argued that only in Christ's experience can the words be
taken literally; in David's they must be metaphorical:

My heart panteth, my strength faileth me;
As for the light of mine eyes, it also is gone from
me. 38:10.

It is noteworthy that the figures of speech throughout the

159

series are grouped around the central metaphor of 'drought' and 'drying up', especially significant with reference to the Righteous Man who was likened to a tree planted by rivers of water. (Psalm 1). Now —

> My moisture is turned into the drought of
> summer. Selah. 32:4.
>
> My bones are consumed. 31:10.
>
> My heart panteth. 38:10.

It is also remarkable to find that during this experience of drought thoughts of God find expression in the imagery of water, not only in Psalm 36, of the present group, but on into the following Book, with Psalm 42:

> As the hart panteth after the water brooks . . .
> My soul thirsteth for God, the living God;

and Psalm 48:

> And Thou shalt make them drink of the river of
> Thy pleasures,
> For with Thee is the fountain of life. (vs. 8,9)

Like the river that Ezekiel describes (Ezek. 47:9-12), its waters bring healing and life. It is also the 'spring of living water' spoken of by Jesus at the well of Samaria, and the abundant waters of Psalm 1. Hence how pregnant with significance they were to the Parched Man who cried 'I thirst', and how poignant the ecstatic exclamation of Psalm 46:4 —

> *There is a river*, the streams whereof make
> glad the city of God!

(NOTE. Although the 42nd psalm is not specifically attributed to David, for it heads a new group 'for the sons of Korah' (Psalms 42-49), these were the singers whom David organized as a choir and for whom he may have composed these psalms. This idea would be substantiated by the fact of continuing imagery of water.)

The details of physical suffering amount to a description of the sort of pangs pertaining to crucifixion: the bones are 'consumed', the life is 'poured out', the 'heart pants', the blood is drained; the light of the eye fades; the speaker feels Himself sinking as the waves and billows go over Him; and He is consumed by the blow of God's hand. (Psalms 32,35,38).

His anguish is greatest at the realization that the blow comes from God's own hand.

> Thy hand was heavy upon me. 32:2.
> Thy wrath . . . Thy sore displeasure . . . 38:1.
> Remove Thy stroke from me: I am consumed by
> the blow of Thine hand. 39:10.

Surely He hath borne our griefs, said the prophet, and carried our sorrows; yet we did esteem Him stricken of God — and so He was, for: It pleased the Lord to bruise Him: He hath put Him to grief; and His soul was made an offering for sin.

After the worst blow had fallen upon His soul, when the shame and the darkness and the heartbreak of desolation had reached full measure with the dereliction, when the magnitude of the punishment was equal only to the horror at its cause, then there comes His conscious acceptance and submission as GOD laid on Him the iniquities of us all. He breathes:

> I opened not my mouth, because Thou didst it. 39:9.

The wrath of God struck Him because He had first volunteered to be man's Redeemer, 'who verily was foreordained before the foundation of the world' (I Pet. 1:20). This is emphasized in the 40th Psalm and taken up in the Epistle to the Hebrews (10:5-20) —

> Sacrifice and offering Thou didst not desire,
> but a body hast Thou prepared me . . .
> then said I, Lo, I come to do Thy will, O my
> God'.

In this psalm we are told how He was bruised for our

iniquities; how He underwent the chastisement of our peace; and with what stripes we are healed.

This brings us to the difficult point of the sense of guilt and the cries for pardon that appear in these psalms, such as 'I acknowledged ... I will confess ... 32:5; mine iniquities ... 38:4, etc. He who knew no sin was made sin for us. (II Cor. 5:21) — this is the only explanation. Though it is true that David loved his God and tried to serve Him with a pure heart, the extreme anguish at the burden of transgressions in certain psalms of this group surpasses human dimensions. These then are the cries of the world's Sin-bearer, and it is to the last degree moving to realize that the spiritual anguish of Jesus on the Cross was intensified by the feeling that He had Himself offended the Being most dear to Him. The 'strong crying and tears' of which the writer to the Hebrews speaks (Heb. 5:7-) are here; they are addressed 'unto Him that was able to save Him from death' — that is, eternal death — and (He) was heard in that He feared.

In these psalms we hear the Saviour acknowledge and confess the sins laid upon Him as though they were His own. It is the High Priest confessing the sins of the people on the Day of Atonement (Lev. 16:21). So truly did the burden of man's sin lie upon the Christ of God during those awful hours on the Cross, that of Him the full payment of the account was exacted. He paid for that which He had not taken. (69:4). Illumined by these psalms we are led to realize more vividly the totality of His identification with man as He bore our sins in His own body on the tree (I Pet. 2:22-24). Our heart, moved to adoration, cries: If ever I loved thee, Lord Jesus, 'tis now!'

'... in His own body on the tree ...' When we read of the moral anguish and hear the pleas for pardon in the light of these words from Peter's Epistle, we can more fully understand what it meant to Him to 'bear our sins Himself'. O Lord, He cries (Psalm 38) —

> Rebuke me not in Thy wrath
> Neither chasten me in Thy hot displeasure ...
> Mine iniquities are gone over my head:
> As an heavy burden they are too heavy for me.

And Psalm 41:12 — Mine iniquities have taken hold upon me,

> So that I am not able to look up:
> They are more than the hairs on my head.

Yea, verily, for they were the sins of the world, and behold, they were laid on the spotless Lamb of God that He might purge them away.

The horror of sin to His unaccustomed soul is expressed in nauseating terms —

> There is no soundness in my flesh because of
>   Thine anger . . .
> My wounds stink and are corrupt:
> My loins are filled with a loathsome disease;
> And there is no soundness in my flesh. (38:1,3,5,7).

It is as though the Speaker sees Himself as a leper in God's sight. It is in these extreme terms that one at last comprehends the meaning of 'the Lord laid upon Him the iniquity of us all' (Isa. 53:6). He did not carry it away as it were at arm's length, nor by divine command dismiss our sins: He *bore* them. In these psalms He is 'bowed down greatly' (38:6); He prays to be delivered from 'all my transgressions' (39:8); and, as Peter says, He committed Himself to Him that judgeth righteously.' (I Pet. 2:23).

In Psalm 32 He tells how 'I acknowledged my sin unto Thee, and mine iniquity have I not hid. I said, I will confess my transgressions unto the Lord; and *Thou forgavest* the iniquity of my sin. Selah. (32:5). This, then, was the process by which our sins were done away. The redemption was by His blood; the purging of our sins by His personal substitution, and at His request they were forgiven. In that He rose again we know that the sins He bore had been cleansed, but He underwent the full punishment for them in that He died. What depth in the portrayal of His suffering on Calvary is perceptible by thus reading these psalms of contrition and supplication! For 'verily He took not on Him the nature of angels; but He took on Him the seed of Abraham' and was made like unto His brethren (Heb.

2:16). And after He had 'made reconciliation for the sins of the people' (Heb. 2:17) He could exclaim in the words of Psalm 32:1 —

> Blessed is he whose transgression is forgiven, whose
> sin is covered;
> Blessed is the man unto whom the Lord imputeth
> not iniquity.

The whole debt was paid, and man could go free by believing on Christ as His substitute. Jesus could say for himself as well as for those He redeemed: 'Thou art my hiding-place; . . . Thou shalt compass me about with songs of deliverance'. (32:7) and Psalm 40:6 —

> This poor man cried and the Lord saved him out
> of all his troubles.

There is a new significance in the words —

> The righteous cry, and the Lord heareth, and
> delivereth them.

He had gone down on their behalf to the 'pit' of death, and God —

> . . . inclined unto me and heard my cry;
> He brought me up out of an horrible pit, out of
> the miry clay,
> And set my feet upon a rock . . .
> He hath put a new song into my mouth, even
> praise unto our God. (40:1-3)

He had prayed to be vouchsafed the resurrection (30:8-11) and again in 41:10 'Be merciful unto me, raise me up'. This had been conceded, for God is faithful that promised. By faith Jesus went to the Cross and by faith He rose again with glory and honour.

The 'new song' that was put into His mouth was His thanksgiving for deliverance and for the Resurrection. Deliverance from death because He had won pardon; thanksgiving for that pardon, which meant that His mission on earth was accomplished; raised up so that men might have the witness. God 'spake and it was done; He commanded and it stood fast. The Lord bringeth the counsel of the heathen to nought. He maketh the device of the people of none effect. (vs. 9,10) The 'heathen' had said, 'Take ye Him and crucify Him'; and the 'people' had clamoured: Crucify! He was nailed to the Tree and His body placed in a tomb, 'whom God raised up, having loosed the pains of death: because it was not possible that he should be holden of it,' . . . for David speaketh concerning Him: Therefore did my heart rejoice . . ., moreover also, My flesh shall rest in hope . . . Thou wilt not leave my soul in hell, neither wilt thou suffer Thine Holy One to see corruption. Thou shalt make me full of joy with Thy countenance. (Psalm 16:8-11; Acts 2:24-27). The assurance of resurrection was His before He died; the joy and the new song came as He rose again. His grief and anguish turn into peace and joy at the life won by his sacrifice, as the prophecy had said:

> When Thou shalt make of His soul an offering for
> sin He shall . . . see of the travail of
> His soul and be satisfied. (Isa. 53).

In Romans 8 the same corollary is given, and it is also in these psalms.

The cry of grief and plea for deliverance is succeeded by the 'new song'. Exclamations like the following are interspersed among those of anguish and almost invariably it is the song of joy with which the psalm closes.

> Thou shalt compass me about with songs of
> deliverance. 38:7.

> Be glad and rejoice in the Lord, ye righteous;
> And shout for joy all ye that are upright in
> heart 32.11.

> The angel of the Lord . . . delivereth them. 34:7.

> My soul shall be joyful in the Lord;
> It shall rejoice in His salvation. 35:9.

I will give Thee thanks in the great congregation;
I will praise Thee among much people.

My tongue shall speak of Thy righteousness
And of Thy praise all the day long. 35:28.

The whole of Psalm 33 is a song of thanksgiving for a great deliverance, and the series ends with a mighty Hallelujah:

Blessed be the Lord God of Israel
From everlasting to everlasting. Amen and amen. 41:13.

Such expressions of joy, gratitude and praise are particularly the fruit of the travail of His soul, but He has acquired other wealth in addition. From the spiritual anguish there has arisen a new understanding of God's mercy, a new kind of hope is born, there exists a different and more touching relationship with God. Blessed (O how happy!) is he whose transgression is forgiven, whose sin is covered. (32:1).

He praises God that the children of men may share in His victory. He understands their need for mercy, and rejoices that they too may have life, light, and peace.

How excellent is Thy loving kindness, O God!
Therefore the children of men put their trust
        under the shadow of Thy wings . . .
With Thee is the fountain of life.

In Thy light shall we see light. (36:7,9,10).

Mark the perfect man and behold the upright:
For the end of that man is peace. (37:7;
        cf Psalm 15.)

He testifies to others of God's goodness, and gets them to join in His praise:

O magnify the Lord with me, and let us exalt His
        name together.
I sought the Lord, and He heard me, and
        delivered me . . .

166

... O taste and see that the Lord is good;
Blessed is the man that trusteth in Him. (34:3,4,8).

My soul shall be joyful in the Lord:
It shall rejoice in His salvation. (35:9).

Thy mercy, O Lord, is in the heavens,
And Thy faithfulness reacheth unto the clouds.
The righteousness is like the great mountains:
Thy judgments are a great deep. (36:6).

Let such as love Thy salvation say continually,
The Lord be magnified. (40:16).

If the sins to be confessed were more than the hairs of His head, (42:12), He can later say, still as Man —

Many, O Lord my God, are Thy wonderful works
        which Thou hast done
And Thy thoughts which are to usward;
They cannot be reckoned up in order unto Thee;
If I would declare and speak of them,
They are more than can be numbered. (40:50).

Praise and thanksgiving are also offered that God has been found faithful and His Word had been proved true:

Sing unto Him a new song; play skilfully with a loud
        noise.
For the word of the Lord is right; and all His works
        are done in truth.
Let all the inhabitants of the world stand in awe of
        Him,
For He spake and it was done; He commanded and
        it stood fast.
The counsels of the Lord stand for ever . . .
Our hearts shall rejoice in Him because we have
        trusted in His name. 33:3-21.

It was David who composed these psalms, but their suffering and joy vicariously reveal the exercised soul of Christ. In Psalm 34 he tells what he had learned through the trial;

The angel of the Lord encampeth round about
    them that fear Him and delivereth
    them,
O taste and see that the Lord is good: blessed is the
    man that trusteth in Him. 34:7,8.
The Lord is nigh unto them that are of a broken
    heart and saveth such as be of a
    contrite spirit. 34:18.

In summary;

I sought the Lord and He heard me,
and delivered me from all my fears. 34:4.

David exclaims in wonder at that aspect of God's character which has been revealed:

How excellent is Thy loving kindness, O God!

For Jesus the exclamation was joy at God's mercy shown for His forgiveness made available to man by the door opened into the habitations of God —

They (the children of men) shall be abundantly satisfied
    with the fatness of Thy house;
And Thou shalt make them drink of the river of Thy
    pleasures.
For with Thee is the fountain of life . . . 36:7-9.

These are not so much promises of God as exultant statements of the believer after personal experience and therefore of assurance that it will be equally true for all.

The speaker in these psalms has learned the important lesson that, contrary to what was supposed, the righteous do suffer, but are delivered. 34:19. Though he fall, he shall not be utterly cast down. 37:24. And that the evildoers appear prosperous but shall eventually perish. 34:21. As a consequence of this view of things comes the great 37th psalm:

Fret not thyself.

What assurance, what conviction born of experience rings through it! There is no need to fret at the eclipse of the righteous for it is temporary:

He shall bring forth thy righteousness as the light,
And thy judgment as the noonday . . .
The meek shall inherit the earth
And shall delight themselves in the abundance of
      peace . . .
The Lord forsaketh not His saints —

and so on. The speaker is eager to convey to fellow-sufferers all the wealth that He has brought back from His experience. He calls them together to listen to His wisdom:

Come, ye children, hearken unto me. I will teach
      you the fear of the Lord. 34:11.

The Beatitudes and teachings of Christ in the Sermon on the Mount (Matt. 5-7), so reminiscent of this psalm, end also with the invitation to come and learn of Him.

These psalms were born of some transcendental experience and contain, as we have seen, expressions of profound anguish and physical pain, but dominating these is the tone of thanksgiving, praise and joy arising out of the very anguish. Set in the frame of Gethsemane and Calvary, they reflect the Messiah's thoughts and emotions as He received that intolerable burden of sin and paid man's ransom. But we receive the impression that the agony, both moral and physical, profound as it was, is temporary; the joy goes on for eternity. The purging was accomplished by One Person; the benefit is for mankind. In summary, then, they present the portrait of the Redeemer in the act of redemption and tell of His joy in fulfilling the purposes of God to make the blessing of eternal life accessible to all the human race, to 'whosoever believeth'!

The Righteous Man is the centre of the picture. The several echoes of Psalm 1 prove it and are worth noting:

I delight to do Thy will, O my God:
Yea, Thy law is within my heart. — 40:8.

169

The law of His God is in his heart;
And none of his steps shall slide. — 37:30,31.

This is the Righteous and Perfect Man of Psalms 1 and 15, recognizable as the same who taught and wrought in the Gospels, Jesus the Son of God.

The wicked and evildoers are spoken of in contrast, at whose head is the individual wicked one.

The wicked (singular) flattereth himself in his own
    eyes . . .
The words of his mouth are iniquity and deceit . . .
    He deviseth mischief upon his bed;
He setteth himself in a way that is not good
He abhorreth not evil. (36:2-4).

Note the antithetical parallel with the doings of the Righteous Man of Psalms 1 and 15. In the first psalm evildoers are like chaff; in 35:5 the image is repeated; here they shall be cut down like grass and wither as the herb. (37:2); they shall be cut off (v. 9) and their seed cut off (v. 28); the transgressors shall be destroyed together. (v. 38). The prayer is made that their way be dark and slippery; that the angel of the Lord persecute (pursue?) them (35:5,6) and that they be clothed with shame and dishonour (35:26); they shall perish (37:20) and consume away like smoke.

The Righteous Man in anguish prayed God to 'Plead my cause' (35:1) and to 'stand up for my help (35:2); He has cried to God for protection and vindication against the Wicked One and his followers (35:1-6,22-26) because they rejoiced in his adversity (35:15-19) and God answered that prayer. The thrilling joy with which he tells of that answer vibrates through these psalms which seem to pulsate with the very heartbeat of the Saviour. It is beautiful to think of His rejoicing as He surveyed an accomplished redemption and knew that He had healed the breach between God and man. It is very touching also to realize that much of His joy lies in the fact that He can now share with man His unique privilege — eternal life spent in the eternal home in the presence of the Holy and loving God. He can now say, Behold I, and the children whom the Lord hath given me.

(Isaiah 8:18; Hebrews 2:13).

This joy flows over into BOOK II and it is the theme of the next series of psalms up to psalm 50. If the story of the Nativity tells of the angels' and the shepherds' joy at God's gift to men of a Saviour, the resurrected Reedemer in the Psalms tells of His own joy in the gift to men of eternal life.

Finally, one may speculate on the possibility that the verse:

They looked unto him and were lightened —

or, '. . . their faces grew radiant,' refers to the joy of the waiting souls in Sheol as they beheld their Deliverer. He declares (40:9,10) —

I have preached righteousness in the great
    congregation . . .
I have declared Thy faithfulness and Thy
    salvation.

This seems to refer to the act of which Peter tells (I Pet. 3:14) — 'being put to death in the flesh, but quickened by the Spirit: by which also He went and preached unto the spirits in prison'. Perhaps it is 'the spirits in prison' who are the 'Great congregation' — a euphemism for the dead . . . Isaiah 9:2 prophetically tells how; 'they that dwell in the land of the shadow of death, upon them hath the light shined.' That Light was the presence of the 'Kinsman Redeemer' when He came to the spirits in prison with the message of liberation.

Jesus said of Himself, I am the Light of the world. Eternal light surrounds His Person, and He proclaimed His identity in the synagogue as the One who was sent to 'open the blind eyes, to bring out the prisoners from the prison, and them that sit in darkness out of the prison house' (Isa. 42:7; 61:1,2; Luke 4:17-21). To them Jesus might have said in the words of Isaiah to Israel: 'Arise, for thy light is come, and the glory of the Lord is risen upon thee.' (60:1). And this Light came and shone also on us, as Paul says to the Colossians — '. . . giving thanks unto the Father which hath made us to be partakers of the inheritance of the saints in light: Who hath delivered us from the power of darkness, and hath translated us into the kingdom of His dear Son.' (Col. 1:12,13). It is that same light of which the psalmist speaks (36:9) — 'In thy light shall we see light'. The Righteous man concludes this series of psalms about the Passion with the words:

> And as for me, Thou upholdest me in my
>   integrity:
> And settest me before Thy face for ever. 41:12.

The author or scribe concludes the book with:

> Blessed be the Lord God of Israel from everlasting
>   to everlasting. Amen and amen.

The alternating pattern of light and shade, sorrow and joy, in this series of psalms (31-41) becomes evident by making a brief outline of each and reading the whole consecutively. It could be entitled, The Act of Redemption. Of these eleven psalms, nine are in the first person, and comprise a personal account of the depths and heights traversed by Our Saviour and Redeemer, the sent One of God, as He carried out His assignment.

If Mark's Gospel contains the incidents which illumine the earlier Psalms (1-24), the parallels of thought that can be traced between the present group (31-41) and the Gospel of John are quite remarkable. John's Gospel more than any of the others reports the discourses and prayers of Jesus, thus giving an account of His mind's working. These psalms fill in many parts of that account which were not spoken or not reported and give its more intimate side. The incidents reported in the first half of that Gospel, some of them exclusive to it, are illustrative of the main thoughts and more striking imagery of these psalms, as for instance, the Light of the world, the Water of life, the Life, and others. The more obvious parallels amount to at least seventy-seven! There is also much that corresponds to events recorded in the Gospel of Luke, the most striking being the Seventh Cry from the Cross (Psalms 31:5). The major part of the content of Psalms 31 to 41 seems, however, to fit the possible thoughts, spiritual anguish and prayers of the Saviour during the hours when the price of our redemption was being paid, for it must be acknowledged that all in these psalms cannot be attributed literally to David's own experience alone. There is no doubt, as in every poet's work, a part of the author's personal experience is woven into it, but since we believe that all Scripture is given by inspiration of God, it is surely lawful to believe that the Holy Spirit led David to put into human language emotions and spiritual experiences far beyond his own, as when David writes: They pierced my hands and feet. (Psalm 22:16). We are trying to place ourselves imaginatively in the situation of Jesus, not David, and see how the exclamations of joy and sorrow, prayer and spiritual wrestling, agony and exultation, may correspond with what probably could have been of Jesus in the events recorded in the Gospels. David knew and in faith apprehended that the Messiah must come of his seed.

With Psalm 41 we come to the end of BOOK I of the Psalms. As the concluding psalm of the series it is remarkable in that in spite of its subject being of deepest sorrow, it opens with the blessing on a man whom the Lord has delivered and closes with 'Blessed be the Lord for ever'. Deeper experience brings greater praise. In the sequence from Psalm 30 that experience for the Incarnate Son was the road to the Cross and His sacrifice thereon, out of which was born life more abundant for those whom His death redeemed. He had pleased the Father and brought glory and praise to His name. And He can say —

As for me, Thou upholdest me in mine integrity,
And settest me before Thy face for ever. (41:12).

As we look back, what strikes us most forcibly is the fact that these psalms, written by David and often connected with events in his own life (as annotated in the superscriptions), nevertheless present a portrait of the mind and personal experience of Christ, and further, cover the period of His messianic mission from its inception to the act of redemption at its close, culmination with the Resurrection and the Ascension in almost chronological sequence, the greater emphasis and detail being of the final hours, roughly in the same proportion as in John's Gospel.

A review of the information gleaned from the study of the First Book of Psalms as applicable to the thoughts of Christ and in the setting of His earthly envionment and experiences, shows the following:

Each stage of His Messiahship as Redeemer is covered, both those recorded in the Gospels, i.e. visible to the narrator and hence external, and those unrecorded because they existed only in His intimate experience and were neither related by Him to anyone nor witnessed by any human being. These consist of prayer and supplication to God; personal emotions of hope, dread, fear, relief, pain and joy, human suffering and exaltation; expressions of (private) anguish, and outbursts of praise with thanksgiving for prayer heard, i.e. for deliverance and victory. In synthesis they record His communings with God and the effect on His spirit on His intercourse with God and with men. All of these are in accordance with the Scriptures written about Him, either by the prophets, in Old Testament types, or in the setting of the Gospel narratives. The private experiences are spoken of in the Psalms of David not so much prophetically as in an impersonation by which, under the inspiration of the Holy Ghost, David's spirit identified itself with the Messiah's and speaks or suffers accordingly.

Some of the Messianic experences are not of this earth: they take place in Heaven and in Hell, and are therefore beyond the ken of man, but have been revealed through David's songs and prayers though veiled under his authorship. Their identification with events in the life of Christ is attested by the apostolic discourses and revelations. The following is an outline of these.

I. Events in the Life of Christ which the Gospels do not tell.

A. In Heaven before His birth:
1. The decree of His Sonship. Psalm 2.
2. His volunteering to be the Redeemer and His commission for the task of Redemption. Psalm 40:6-8; Psalm 2.
3. His Personality described or presented. Psalms 1, 15, 18;20-29; 27.

B. In Hell (after physical death) period while He was absent from the body. Psalms 23;40.
1. His descent into Hell: Psalms 22; 40; 18:4-6, 16-19.
2. His prayer for protection and help for His task: Psalms 22:19; 27:9; 28:2; 30:10.
3. His activities there: Psalms 18:32-42, 47, 48.
4. His prayer for deliverance: Psalms 22:20,21; 25:20; 40:13.
5. His prayer for resurrection. Psalms 21:2-4; 30:9,10; 39;13.
6. Message of encouragement to the believers' spirits confind there: Psalms 32:11; 34:22.
7. Rescue of the righteous spirits in Sheol. Psalms 34:5; 36:9.
8. Preaching to the congregation in Sheol. Psalms 35:18; 40:9,10; 22:22.
9. Distinction between two groups of spirits there: Those who looked for Him and those who repudiated Him.
10. Description of the place: Psalms 40:2,12,14,15; 18:4,5,16,17.

C. The Resurrection and after.
   On earth: Psalms 24:1-6.
   In Heaven: His return to the Father. 24:7-10.

II. Experiences and Emotions during Jesus' life on earth about which the Gospels are not explicit.

A. Caused by His observation of the Creation: the

firmament, the heavenly bodies, nature (animate and inamate), the elements, etc. Psalms 8, 18, 19, 29.

B. Caused by His observation of human nature and its behaviour:
1. The godly: Psalms 1, 9, 15, 16, 20, 21, 24, 26, 33, 34, 37, 40, 41.
2. The ungodly; Psalms 2, 3, 5, 7, 10, 11, 12, 14, 17, 36, 41.

C. Caused by the impact of these on His personal feelings: Psalms 4, 6, 13, 18:1-6, 16-50; 22, 23, 25, 26, 27, 28, 30, 31, 32, 35, 38, 39, 40.

III.   The Passion:-

A. Reported in the Gospels.
False witnesses, accusations, mock trial:
Psalms 5:9, 10; 27:12; 28:3; 31:13, 18; 35:1, 7, 11, 19; 37:14; 38:12, 19; 41:5-9.
Betrayal. Psalm 41:9.
Crucifixion. Psalm 22.
The hours on the Cross: Psalms 6, 13, 19, 31, 32, 33, 34, 35, 38, 39.

B. Behind the scenes.
Petitions for mercy and help; expressions of sorrow and grief. 31, 38.
The Dereliction: Psalms 22:1; 27:9; 30:5, 7.
Bearing and 'declaring' or 'confessing' the guilt laid on Him: Psalms 25:11; 38.
Praise and gratitude for sins purged, forgiveness received: Psalms 18:28, 30, 33, 36, 40; also found in Psalms 7, 9, 10, 12, 13, 16, 22, 27, 31, 34, 35, 41.

C. The Resurrection.
1. Period while He was absent from the body. Psalms 23, 40.
2. Return to take up the body. Psalms 24:1-6. II Sa., 23:4, 5.

3.   Physical resurrection. Psalms 2:7; 16:10; 18:19-30.

This proves His final and total victory over evil:
a. over Death, hence over Satan and satanic powers
    — proving that He is LIFE.
b. cover the hypocritical leaders and false teaching —
    proving that He is TRUTH.
c. over fear, doubt and dejection in the hearts of His
    people — proving that He is the WAY.

D. Expressions of joy and gratitude to God for His victory
and the answer to His prayer for deliverance and
resurrection: Psalms 18:29-50; 17:15; 27; 28:6-9; 30.

It will be noted that the Psalms reveal in more detail than
the Gospels that Christ was constantly aware of reality in
three spheres simultaneously: Heaven, Earth, and Hell.
They also reveal His character and behaviour on the three
planes, with relation to God, man, and Satan. His enemies
are threefold, too: Satan and evil spirits, acting with
subtlety and deadly intent. The hypocritical leaders, acting
with violence and hatred. The multitude who act with
fickleness or indifference in spite of knowing that He had
done good to so many.

The human life of the Messiah, our Lord Jesus, as seen in
the Psalms, is exactly as described by Paul —
1. With relation to God— He experienced His love and
mercy; He was raised up and given the seat at God's right
hand; and in the ages to come, He will, with His redeemed
ones, proclaim the exceeding riches of God's grace. (Eph.
2:4-10)
2. With regard to humanity. He was Perfect Man ('the
stature of the fulness of Christ'); He loved us and gave
Himself an offering and a sacrifice to God on man's behalf.
(Eph. 4:13 and 5:2).
3. With regard to Satan. He met the wiles of the devil;
He wrestled with spiritual wickedness in high places. (Eph.
6:10-18).

The most startling single fact to emerge from the Messianic interpretation of the First Book of the Psalms is that Jesus the Christ on earth did not act in self-sufficiency, but constantly sought aid from the Father and was entirely dependent on Him for guidance. This brings the revelation that the true believer literally lives the Christian life, i.e. the kind of life that Christ lived on earth, and if he has to plead with God with strong crying and tears, he need not feel that this infers the existence of an impediment in himself such as lapsed communion or poverty of the spiritual life, for thus did the Master plead.

A complete picture of the inner life of Christ can be pieced together from these psalms, parts of which we have recapitulated at various stages. With unsuspected detail it rounds out the Character and Personality of Jesus Christ as presented in the Gospels, and offers a remarkably complete portrait of the Son of God.

In prayer as seen in the Psalms Christ cried, He wrestled, He wept, He worshipped, He praised, He denounced sinners, He pled for His life. But he never prayed that His death might be acceptable. That the Sacrifice would be accepted was undoubted, because He was sinless. When He said, 'Lo, I come', His voluntary offering was made and accepted once and for all; accepted in Eternity when He made the offer; accepted in time present while He fulfilled it, and accepted as valid when He returned to God, for all Eternity to come. He did not pray on earth: 'Let my sacrifice be acceptable in Thy sight', because His offering was not of His own devising, but like that of Abel, it was an act of obedience. The fact that He was there was His service. But He did pray that the goal might be reached successfully, and that God's plan for Him might be carried out faithfully. This shows His recognition of the power and determination of His arch-enemy to frustrate or neutralize the validity of His offering and obstruct the winning of His goal. It also shows that He felt the need for God's help and guidance, and that He trusted in the Father's power as supreme.

PORTRAIT OF CHRIST AS SEEN IN BOOK ONE OF THE PSALMS

The Book opens with a character sketch of the Blessed Man whose chief delight is meditation in God's Law, and at the close comes His own statement concerning His delight in doing the will of God. This was the purpose for which He offered Himself to the Father for the act of Redemption.

As the 'tree planted by rivers of water', He enjoyed fullness of life both outwardly and inwardly, that is, physically and spiritually He was at the peak of health. Full of energy, He was purposeful in deed and forthright in word; vigorous and enthusiastic in His commitment; His spirit hopeful; radiating life but His manner serene with inner peace and quiet joy.

Loving God and delighting in His Word as totally as He did, He expected the norm that ruled His life to rule others also, and was astonished to find that this was not so. Conscious of His own rectitude toward God, He was at first pained by the rebuffs He received from the malice of the religious leaders, but their harshness served only to strengthen His determination to declare God's willingness to bless. His indignation was aroused by men's falseness, wilful evil, and indifference, and He denounced them to their faces.

He could be gentle, compassionate and sympathetic, but when occasion arose, He showed firmness, moral strength and innate majesty. Capable of anger and indignation, He evinced this only when God rather than Himself was dishonoured or slighted. (cf Luke 12:10).

His look could be commanding, at times even of stern authority, but He was easily entreated by the needy. He was never haughty, though He held Himself with dignity and His natural air of command was compelling. Sometimes, according to the Gospels, this might be shown by a look, a word, or gesture.

Highly strung, He was more sensitive than average but exercised self control and had firm command over both His anger and His tears. He often wept and His heart was sore, but His character was serene, His eyes illuminated by secret joy.

He had great courage. He knew the powers and the wiles of His adversaries, both demonic and human, but He challenged them boldly and did battle with them, winning the contest by apt application of God's Word rather than by force of argument or eloquence. His well chosen replies discomfited His opponents, whether their attacks were overt or sly, but secretly He often had recourse to prayer for wisdom, strength and guidance and for comfort and reassurance.

He showed resolute determination and decision; was persevering and experienced endurance both moral and physical. He was patient with the weak and ignorant, and also when instructing His disciples, but was unflinching and downright in His denunciation and condemnation of the men who wilfully and persistently set God aside, the hypocrites and the pretentious.

His nature was attune with God and with Creation. He loved the mountains and fields, husbandry and the fruitfulness of the soil, the countryside and the sight of the sea. Thunder was as the voice of God and a storm or tempest an exhibition of His power and dominion, and He was uplifted by the sight of a starry sky, the moon and the sun. He often made use of nature for illustrations of God's mysteries. (Jesus' recorded speech is full of natural imagery). His mind could take in at a glance a world of beauty and His enjoyment found expression in praise, magnifying God the Creator.

Thoughtful by inclination and a lover of silent meditation, He inwardly shrank from the vociferous crowds, but He was not a recluse and did not shun the company of men; on the contrary, He went out to meet them or sought them out in order to help them on the way to God. He liked to gather them around Him to instruct them in the knowledge of God, often drawing from his own experience to point the lesson.

He loved His country and the land. He felt one with his nation and His heart embraced also the heathen around Him. He was not a nationalist or a racialist. Mankind was classified in His mind into the two categories of men who loved and sought God, and those who hated and disobeyed Him. He loved the Temple and often went there. (The Gospels add that He frequented the synagogue as well).

He loved God above all, and had recourse to Him at all times for every contingency (not only emergencies!). His communion with His Father was the most precious thing in his life. He loved the members of His human family but gave them up when He was called to public service, reserving Himself for God alone. (The Gospel adds that he even repudiated family ties and home when faced with the choice). He loved the men who had left all to follow him because they sought to do the will of God; He called them his brethren, but even from this love He was cut off when He needed its support. He was encouraged to persevere by the vision of bringing to the Father a very large family, Himself being the Firstborn of many bretheren.

Though true Man, He was continually aware of two others realms — Heaven, the habitation of God, and the satanic kingdom of darkness. He could see angels and demons. He was as aware of the devil's siege of His Person as He was of God's Presence in Him. His confidence was not in His own power; He trusted God to preserve Him and give Him the final victory by restoring Him to life and the position He had first held before the calamaties came upon Him (interpreted in terms of the Gospel story, this referred to His death and resurrection).

The feeling of weakness or exhaustion seems to have surprised Him. When on the Cross bearing the world's sin, He made complaint of His physical suffering as though He had expected to go through the ordeal without physical disability. From this we gather that He could feel weariness but had never known illness. Also, that the human state was explored gradually by the divine Son as events progressed.

His high calling and the purpose of His mission was ever

before Him; all His thoughts were oriented towards it, including the importance of keeping His body without blemish from the cruel intent of His enemies but the thought of His death, far from depressing him, brought joy on two counts: one, that by it He would be fulfilling the will of His God; the other that He would bring eternal life to man. He was not indifferent to danger any more than he was to the power of evil, but he braved both, sometimes with human trepidation but always through prayer confident that God would bring Him through so that his task would be completed. For this He was dependent upon God at every stage.

His mind is of quite unusual power and fortitude, but He was capable of being tempted. His manner was an amalgam of humility and boldness; His spirit knew both fear and trust, anguish and elation. He could go through the most severe testing with equanimity so long as He felt the approval of the Father; and His mind's eye was habitually fixed on an event in the far future (which sometimes He speaks of as though it were present) in which by faith He sees His reign on earth in power and glory and the vindication of the truth of His teachings and hence the veracity of God's Word.

His soul worships God; He acknowledges the Father's supremacy, yet his natural way of thinking is absolutely one with the divine, He being of one substance with the Father. He is shown to be both divine Son of God, and Son of Man, knowing the thoughts of God yet delighting in the study of His Law day and night.

At the consummation of his sacrificial act on the Cross He underwent the most total anguish of body and spirit but when the dark cloud of God's wrath had spent itself and the sins that were laid on him were purged and forgiven, serenity and peace returned and He went down to "the pit" (Sheol) trusting in God to raise him up again. His joy at the fulfilment of His mission and the answer to his supplication is coloured by generosity and love, praise and thanksgiving, vivid as the colours of the rainbow. He expresses His joy in exultant cries of blessing on all men who seek God and rejoices in anticipation of the benefits His earthly rule will bring, for He has wrested the sceptre from the grasp of his enemy Satan and will govern with peace, bringing even the heathen under his peaceful sway. (There is greater emphasis on this aspect in BOOK II).

The final note and the sum total of His human existence is:

> O magnify the Lord with me, and let us exhalt
> His name together

Some of these characteristics were also David's as discerned in the psalms he wrote and in the account of his life and character; but most of them transend the human and are undeniably those of the Messiah he was unknowingly portraying. They are all borne out by what we know of Jesus the Christ through the Gospel records. It is only after reading the First Book of the Psalms in this light that we are able to appreciate the hidden third dimension of such passages as Philippians 2:5-11. With their help we can see "the mind of Christ" at work and apprehend something of *His* side of the picture. 'Let this mind be in you, which was also in Jesus Christ who, being in the form of God, thought it not robbery to be equal with God, but made Himself of no reputation, and took upon Him the form of a servant, and was made in the likeness of men: and being found in fashion as a man, He humbled Himself and became obedient unto death, even the death of the cross. Wherefore God also hath highly exalted Him, and given Him a name which is above every name: that at the name of Jesus every knee should bow ... and that every tongue should confess that Jesus Christ is Lord, to the glory of God the Father.'

It helps one to approach an answer to the question: How far was He man while in the flesh. We learn from these psalms that He divested Himself of divine prerogative while on earth, and from the Gospels that He only made use of his divine power when required to do so for the glory of God. He accepted physical limitations but was in a truly literal sense God Incarnate, evincing a mind divine inhabiting a body truly human.

INDEX TO BOOK ONE

EPILOGUE

In these Psalms we see how Jesus Christ the Son of God 'worked out (His) salvation with fear and trembling', 'doing the will of God from the heart'. He stood, having His loins girt about with truth and wearing the breastplate of righteousness; His 'feet shod with the preparation of the gospel of peace', and with the shield of faith He was able to quench all the fiery darts of the evil one. Though He was the Image of the Invisible and in Him dwelt all the fullness of the Godhead bodily, He prayed with supplication in the Spirit, watching thereunto with all perseverance. Thus His patience and long suffering were with joyfulness and He was strengthened with glorious power.

By faith He sojourned in the land of promise as in a strange country, for He looked for a city whose builder and maker is God. In everything He was an ensample to the flock. As He is, so are we in this world. All that we have been enjoined to be or do He was and did first: — in much patience, in afflictions, in necessities, in distress ... in labours, in watchings, by pureness, in fastings, by knowledge, by long suffering, by kindness, by the Holy Spirit, by love unfeigned, by the word of truth, by the power of God, by the armour of righteousness; by honour and dishonour, ... as unknown yet well known, as dying and behold we live; as chastened and not killed; as sorrowful yet always rejoicing; as poor and yet making others rich; as having nothing and yet possessing all things.

In whom also we have obtained an inheritance, being predestinated according to the purpose of Him who worketh all things after the counsel of His own will that we should be to the praise of His glory.

References to the above quotations: Phil. 2:12; Eph. 6:6,14-18. Col. 1:15; 2:9; Eph. 6:18; Col. 1:11; Heb. 11:9,10; I Pet. 5:3; I John 4:17; II Cor. 6:1-10; Eph. 1:11,12.

MEDITATIONS
ON THE
MEDITATOR

PSALM 119

Many readings of this psalm are necessary before its meaning is revealed. It is not, as at first it appears to be, merely a collection of devotional sayings around the theme of the devout man's pleasure in the Law of the Lord. The Levites being the custodians of the sacred manuscripts (Deut. 31:9), it would appear to be the work of a Levite. Some commentators believe the author to have been Ezra; Spurgeon suggests David. ('The Treasury of David'). Ezra, a chief Levite with direct descent from Aaron (Ezra 7:1-5; Neh. 12:1), is described as a "ready scribe in the law of Moses" (7:6) and a man who had "prepared his heart to seek the law of the Lord and do it, and to teach Israel statutes and judgments" (7:10; and see Psalm 119:112, 'I have inclined my heart', etc.) His learning is emphasized (v. 11), but we are not told of any occasion on which Ezra was personally the target of the enemy as the author here complains, and certainly not, as in the psalm, for reasons of his love of God's precepts. In Ezra's chapter 9 the "iniquities and trangressions" which cause him anguish had been committed against the Law of the Lord (cf. 119:136), not in persecution of himself. Though such transgressions are mentioned in this psalm, the author cries there to God for assurance and protection from personal attacks of the wicked. (119:21,23, etc.)

In Nehemiah we have a character who was personally discredited and maligned by his enemies and the enemies of

God; he was despised and his acts held in contempt as the psalmist says (v. 141). He also narrates how he appealed to God (Neh. 2:19; 4:4) because "they laughed us to acorn and despised us". Ezra 2:2-8; Neh. 7, etc., however, show that Nehemiah was not a Levite and would presumably not be so familiar with the whole Law as the author of this psalm claims to be. Further, there is no reference to Nehemiah's special dedication to the study of the Law.

However those who study the original text may claim to tell whether it is post-exilic or not through variations in the language, a comparison with certain psalms of David, such as Psalm 25, 31, 39, 64, 69, 139, 143, and others, presents parallels striking enough to cause the speculation that the 119th might have been written by the chief Korahite in David's time, that is, Asaph, (if Levite it must be), but there are several points so close in spirit to David's own, especially the "I am thy servant" plea, that speculation is invited on the author's being David himself, perhaps over a period of years, though to our knowledge he was not persecuted for his adherence to God's Word. On the other hand, Jeremiah, a Levite, was, (Jer. 26), and he is the author of that other acrostic masterpiece, "Lamentations".

In the discourse which was the prelude to the delivering of the Book into the care of the priests, Moses frequently makes use of the terms which are played upon like the strings of a musical instrument in this psalm: the Law of the Lord, His statutes, judgments, commandments, testimonies, words "of His covenant", or "of this Law"; His ways, But strangely enough "precepts" does not appear until Nehemiah 9:14. The words are often coupled in the same way by Moses and by the writer of this psalm. For instance: statutes and judgments (Deut. 4:8; 11:32; 26:16; etc); the commandments of the Lord and His statutes (10:13); the commandments of the Lord and His testimonies (6:17); testimonies and statutes and judgments which the Lord our God hath commanded you. (6:20); keep His commandments and walk in His ways (8:6); all His ways are judgment (32:4). These are only a few taken at random. It is a characterisitc mode of his speech, from which we may gather that it was the Book of Deuteronomy that the writer of the 119th Psalm especially "delighted" in, though it may be supposed that he knew all five books of Moses at least, and he seems to be familiar with the Book of Proverbs, since there are many passages that are similar. The following are some of the most striking:

PSALM 119	PROVERBS	PSALM 119	PROVERBS
v. 3	12:28	v. 112	8:30, 31
v. 5	11:5; 15:10	v. 114	14:26, 27; 18:10
v. 11	22:18	v. 120	14:26, 27
v. 14	9:9	v. 124	9:8, 9; 15;14
v. 30	9:9, 10	v. 127	8:10
v. 42	22:21	v. 128	8:15; 13:5
v. 46	22:20	v. 142	8:20
v. 59	15:19	v. 147	23:17
v. 71	17:10	v. 152	12:28
v. 72; 127	8:10, 19		
v. 99	12:28; 8:2		
v. 105	6:23		

(These are 21 (3 x 7). There may be more.

The structure of the psalm is well known: An alphabetical acrostic with a stanza of eight "verses" to each letter of the Hebrew alphabet. Each biblical "verse" consists of two clauses (rarely three) forming a sort of couplet, not necessarily of parallels.

The general theme at first sight is God's Word and the writer's relation to it, but certain signs of emotion on the part of the author suggest a third element: the occasion which brought forth this eulogy. The pattern therefore is as it were a "brede" of several strands which may be traced as: 1 — The beauties of God's Word; 2 — The blessedness of the devout man who loves to meditate therein; 3 — The sorrows of the righteous man who suffers for his allegiance to it.

The author's main emotion is his devotion to the law of the Lord; his second one is closely mingled with another which sounds very near to hurt or resentment. The blessedness and sorrow are nearly always closely linked together, often in the same sentence, and if the poem is to be seen as such, these factors must be seen in relation to each other. Furthermore, frequently the two parts of a verse do not seem to make sense if the third factor is not taken into account. Examples: v. 23, 39, 51, 61, 69, 83, 95, 109, 110, 119, 127, 141, 149, 157, 176. The conjunction "yet", "but", "therefore", "because", linking the two statements especially point to a fourth element which emerges as an inference that unjust criticism and censure has caused his sorrow. Some examples cited show no apparent logical sequence at all if this fourth factor is not held to be tacitly inferred.

The situation which would make the sequence logical, even significant, is that the author of the psalm is suffering the opprobrium of certain men *because of* his devotion to the law, precepts, judgments, testimonies, etc., of the Lord. It might almost be said that there is a tone of expostulation if not of actual complaint at an injustice persistently received, and there are hints that he faces and expects its repetition in the near future.

The general characteristic of the style is austere simplicity. There are very few adjectives. The only ones used denote the highest moral qualities: *righteous* (v. 8, 62, 106, 160, 164): *good*, v. 39; *faithful*, v. 86, 138; *rightful*, v. 172; *broad* (limitless), v. 96; *sweet*, sweeter, v. 103; *right*, v. 128; *pure*, v. 140; *true*, v. 160 (truth, v. 142); *everlasting*, v. 144: that is, ten, used in only 15 verses out of a total of 176 verses. The only comparisons are: sweeter than honey, and better than gold, i.e. absolutes.

The poem is stripped of all poetic ornaments. There are no flights of prophetic vision; there is no anticipated glory or cry for divine vengeance; no high drama, no extremes of dread or hope accentuate its contrasts; affliction is only mentioned. There is no poetic rapture or excitement except the exclamation, "O how I love thy law!"; no building up to a climax, no deep emotion but a steady love of God's law and the repudiation of evil, this in measured tones. No transports of joy interrupt the even glow of its quiet steady flame of devotion. He "delights" in 'Thy statutes", v. 16, in the "path of Thy commandments", v. 35; and in "Thy law", vs. 70, 77, 92; 174. "Thy testimonies" (24) and "Thy commandments" (143) are said to be the author's "delight". He rejoices in "the way of Thy testimony" (14); "Thy statutes" have been his "songs in the house of my pilgrimage" (54); "Thy testimonies" are "the rejoicing of my heart" (111). These emotions are subdued and spiritual.

When the same word is used several times it is found to apply to each of the various aspects of the Law in turn: he will "meditate", for instance, "in Thy precepts" (15, 78), "statutes" (23, 48), "testimonies" (95), "Thy law" (97), "Thy word" (148), etc. The same has been noted above of his "delight".

But there is sufficient expression of emotion to paint a vibrant and warm personality. "O that my ways were directed to keep Thy statutes!' (5). *"With my whole heart* have I sought Thee. *O let me not* wander from Thy commandments! (10); "with my" or "with the whole heart" occurs in v. 2, 10, 34, 58, 69 and 145; and "diligently" in v. 4. *My soul breaketh* for *longing* . . . (20); *longing* for Thy commandments (131), salvation (174); *my soul cleaveth* to the dust (25); *melteth* for heaviness 828); *fainteth* for Thy salvation (81); my reproach which I *fear* (89); I have *longed for* Thy precepts (40); Thy commandment have I *loved* (48); *Horror* at the ways of the wicked (53, 136); I *hope,* . . . Thou hast made me to hope (81) . . . in Thy word (147, 166). *O how I love* Thy law! (97, 133), . . . testimonies (119), . . . commandments (127). Mine eyes fail for Thy word (82), . . . salvation (123). *How sweet* are Thy words! (103).

Praise of the Law occurs often, and praise of the Lord for His goodness, mercy, faithfulness, righteous judgments, truth, many times (7, 12, 30, 39, 64, 68, 72, 90, 103, 106, 140, 156, 164), in fact he says he praises God seven times a day because of His righteous judgments. (164).

The sorrowful emotions increase towards the latter part of the psalm. His sorrow like his delight, mingles with a cry of protest and a reaffirmation of his knowledge and love of the Law, precepts, judgments, etc. "I was *afflicted"* (71, 75); I *entreated* Thy favour (58); he asks for *comfort* (76, 77, 82); I *beseech* Thee (108); I *hate* every false way (128, 163); "rivers of water" flow from his eyes (136); he is "despised" (141); *trouble* and *anguish* have taken hold on him (143); he *cries* to be heard (145); to be *saved* (146); for *deliverance* (153, 154) and for *mercy* (132); and asks God to *"Plead my cause"* (154); he complains that "many are my *persecutors* and my *enemies* (157), and he is *grieved* when he beholds the transgressors (158). We must add to this list his "delight" and "rejoicing". He finally reaches a plane on which no trouble may touch him — "Great *peace* have they which love Thy law" (165), though he closes with a further cry to God — "Seek Thy servant". v. 176.

Many lines suggest what had caused this unhappiness: his feelings seem at times to be coloured by a sense of injury, for his expressions of devotion to God and love of His Word mingle with protestations of his integrity and of self-vindication against unmerited criticism and persecution. He also prays nine times to be "quickened".

Reasons for his sorrow are mostly suggestive of persecution. No fewer than 66 verses make mention of this, including "reproach" and "enemies", and these are frequently linked, as we have noted above, with expressions of his devotion to the written Word. For example; "The bands of the wicked have robbed me: but I have not forgotten Thy law. (61). "The proud have forged a lie against me, but I will keep Thy precepts with my whole heart" (69). "I am become like a bottle in the smoke, yet do not I forget Thy precepts" (83). "The wicked have waited for me to destroy me: but I will consider Thy testimonies" (95), and so on. He vows to keep "Thy statutes", "Thy word", "Thy words", "Thy law", for ever; "Thy commandments for ever"; "Thy precepts," "Thy testimonies", and "judgments"; and affirms that he has kept the same heretofore. Note here also how the vow is applied to each of the eight words for the sacred writings throughout the psalm. He binds himself to keep them all. "I have sworn and I will perform it, that I will keep Thy judgments" (106); and states that he will keep them "for ever and ever" (44); His testimonies are taken as a heritage for ever (111), because they are "founded for ever" (152). His careful obedience to them is for him a form of worship, as is implied in "I will keep the commandments of my God" (115). A summary of his whole sentiment in the psalm is found in the second section (BETH) — the first stanza being introductory — : Thy word have I hid in my heart (11); Teach me thy statutes (12); I recite them one by one (13); I rejoice in the way of Thy testimonies (14); I will meditate in thy precepts, delight in thy statutes, and will not forget Thy word (13-16). His vows are of fidelity to, constancy in, acceptance of, obedience to, and full-hearted devotion to the Sacred Words. He declares his love for the law, his determination to heed and follow it, and promises a fourfold blessing on all those that seek God and do this with their whole heart. (1,2).

His language is so measured and subdued throughout that when he says (44) "I will keep thy law for ever and ever", we must take it that he means it literally. The reiteration implies his vivid awareness of eternity future. He vows to keep God's law throughout a life discerned as eternal. To do this he must be of that everlasting nature himself, and have knowledge of eternal existence. Thus it shows that a divine mind is at work.

It is therefore interesting to see: a) What the speaker tells us about himself; b) what he knows of God; and c) what he requests of God.

a)   **What the speaker tells us about himself.**

We have already seen that he is a devout lover and follower of the Sacred Precepts, that they are his delight and that he is labouring under the sorrow of persecution. But what does he *tell* us about himself? There are his vows both present and future ("I delight . . ., I will delight myself . . ." "I have kept . . .", "I will keep" . . .) These denote his firm purpose and intention "I have rejoiced", I will meditate" — past, present and future are bound in his mind to the one exercise of furthering his knowledge of the Word of God. But these are intellectual and spiritual activities of any devoted lover of God. We have noted something of his emotions. We have seen his fervent desire to obey and fulfil the law, his warm heartedness, his passion for the statutes and judgments of a holy God, his capacity for deep feeling — "O how I love — !" "Horror hath taken hold on me". "Rivers" of tears. "With my whole heart I sought Thee". "I hate and abhor lying". Further hints of his character may be drawn from his sense of being wronged and his firm resolve to follow the truth. — "Princes did sit and speak against me, but Thy servant did meditate in Thy statutes" (2).

"The wicked have waited to destroy me" (55) . . . "My

soul cleaveth to the dust" (25); "The proud have had me in derision" (51); "Trouble and anguish have taken hold on me" (143), etc.

What do we know of his daily habits and activities? There are few glimpses but they afford vivid details — "Thy word have I hid in my heart that I might not sin against Thee" (11); "With my lips have I declared the judgments of Thy mouth" (13); "Thy statutes have been my songs in the house of my pilgrimage" (54); "I have remembered Thy name in the night" (55); "Mine eyes prevent the night watches" (148); "At midnight will I rise to give thanks unto Thee" (68). We see that he memorizes, speaks, thinks, sings, studies and meditates day and night on God's Word. The present trouble has produced in him *"dread"* (39), *longing*, (40, 20); *hope* (43, 49, 50); *comfort* (at the remembrance of Thy judgments of old) (52, 152); *affliction* (67, 71, 75), *wisdom* (88, 89, 100) and an increased *fear of God* (120). These he declares to be his experience. But what of his *secret feelings?* He does sometimes confess these. They are still rarer and very valuable. The former were inferences; these are direct admissions. From his *private thoughts* he lets drop the following: "I am a stranger in the earth" (19); "I have chosen the way of truth" (30); "I am a companion to those that fear Thee" (63). "They that fear Thee will be glad when they see me" (74); "My soul pines for Thy salvation" ... "I am become like a bottle in the smoke" (83); "Unless Thy law had been my delight I should have perished in my affliction" (82); "I have seen an end to all perfection" (96). "I have hoped for Thy salvation." (166). "I have gone astray like a lost sheep." (176), or "roaming far from home". For a didatic poem these personal references are unusual, even unique.

It is worthy of note that these private admissions about himself, taken in the sequence in which they occur, form an outline of stages in the life of Christ, beginning with His Incarnation and ending with the Cry of Dereliction. They suggest an underlying secret pattern which may be a clue to the poem's true significance.

b) **What the speaker knows of God.**

He knows that it is God who formulated the statutes, laws,

precepts, etc. that he loves; that God can and will teach them to him and give him understanding, and has pledged His word to give him life (17); that God chastens and admonishes in order to ensure perfect conformity to His will; that God keeps His word, which was established from eternity; that God hears and answers prayer and has made him hope and has strengthened him; that God is righteous (37) yet shows merciful loving kindness and tender mercies to them that seek Him (156); that He is good and doeth good (68); that God is his Maker (73) and the Creator of the universe (90), faithful in His dealings with man even in afflicting him; that God has trodden down the wicked, the deceitful and sinners; the speaker also trembles for fear of Him (120); that His judgments are upright, His testimonies are righteous and faithful; His word very pure, His law and commandments are truth; and that God is near him in his need. That is, he knows God as all-embracing Wisdom, Immanent and yet Personal. But this knowledge is bounded by that available to every man through a personal experience of God.

c) **What he requests of God.**

Of petitions there are said to be over seventy. Let us see some of them. First (26) he affirms "Thou heardest me", and the first three requests are in the form of exclamations of desire — for guidance, God's Presence, and for prevention from deviating from the Will of God: O that my ways were directed to keep Thy statutes! (50, and cf. 35, 133); O forsake me not utterly (8); O let me not wander from Thy commandments! (10). His most frequent petition is for understanding and that God might *teach* him: Teach me Thy statutes, Thy judgments, good judgment and knowledge (12, 26, 33, 64, 66, 68, 108, 124, 135). Open my eyes (18), hide not Thy commands (19). And for *vindication*: Remove from me reproach and contempt (22); and from falsehood (29). He asks for life and resurrection. "Quicken me" (ten times) according to Thy word (25, 107, 154), in Thy way (37), in Thy righteousness (40), in Thy loving kindness (88, 159), according to Thy judgments (156); and for *strength* and *endurance*: Uphold me (116); strengthen me

(28); be merciful to me according to Thy word; grant me Thy law (29); let me not be put to shame (31, 116). He often *pleads God's promise*: Stablish Thy word to Thy servant (38); let Thy mercies come also to me according to Thy word, even Thy salvation; Remember Thy word unto Thy servant . . . caused me to hope (48, cf. 52). He entreats God for His favour "with my whole heart" (158) . . . for my comfort (76), . . . that I may live (175-7). He asks *to be defended* against his enemies; Let the proud be ashamed (78); Let not the proud oppress me; Leave me not to my oppressors (121); Deliver me (134, 170). He asks for a *meek and obedient spirit*, malleable in God's hands: Make me to go in the path of Thy commandments (35); Incline my heart to Thy testimonies (36); Turn away mine eyes from beholding vanity; Order my steps in Thy word (133). Sometimes he implores in the form of a question that points to his *intense longing*: When wilt Thou comfort me? (82); How many are the days of Thy servant? (84); When wilt Thou execute judgment? (94, 146); Hold Thou me up and I shall be safe (117); Be surety for Thy servant for good (122); Plead my cause (154); Let Thine hand help me (173). He pleads God's *mercy* and *loving kindness* (124, 132, 149), as well as His *fidelity* to His word (170, 25, 107, 154, 28, 58, 169, 17, 41, 43, 76, 116, 38, etc.); and prays to be heard and accepted (108, 135, 149, 169, 170), sometimes pleading his own integrity and devotion — "Consider how I love Thy precepts", or the fact that he is God's servant. "Thy servant" — his name for himself — occurs 12 times, mostly in connection with God's promise and His dealings (17, 23, 38, 49, 65, 76, 84, 122, 124, 135, 140, 176); example: Deal bountifully with Thy servant, that I may live (17); Thou hast dealt well with Thy servant (65); Remember Thy word unto Thy servant (49) . . . according to Thy word (76). In the Psalms "Thy servant" is always a Messianic identification, as in Isaiah and Zechariah. (See Psalms 116:16; 143:12; etc.).

This man who calls himself "Thy servant" when he addresses God and whose daily occupation is the delight and meditation in God's Word, makes certain affirmations about himself that clearly associate him with the Righteous Man of Psalm 1. "O how I love Thy law, it is my meditation all the day . . . and night, preventing the night watches, at midnight (148) and in the dawning (147). Thy law is my delight. I have refrained my feet from the evil way (97); I have not departed from Thy judgment (102); I have kept Thy testimonies; I delight in Thy statutes" (116); and he refuses to associate with the ungodly, the sinners and the scornful, or be contaminated by participating in the activities of the wicked. "Depart from me, ye evildoers" (115). He will "run the way of Thy commandments" (32), while others "sit" and forge lies against Him. He knows that the ungodly shall not stand in the judgment — "Thou puttest away all the wicked of the earth" (119); and looks forward to the time when he will be welcomed in the congregation of the righteous (74).

The central figure of this autobiographical psalm answers to the description of *the Just Man* of Psalm 1 and of the *Righteous and Wise Man* of the Book of Proverbs, as also to *the Servant* in Isaiah and Zecharaiah. An eye-witness of the behaviour of Jesus under provocation is to be found in I Pet. 2:19-23 — ". . . if, when ye do well and suffer for it, ye take it patiently, this is acceptable with God . . . Christ also suffered . . . who did no sin . . . and when He was reviled, reviled not again; when He suffered He threatened not; but committed Himself to Him that judgeth righteously . . ." which also remarkably coincides with the Nature of the Man who is the Speaker in this Psalm.

Let us now try to distinguish what may have been the cause of this upright man's distress. Summarizing the information we have gathered we find that:

1. He seems to have been the victim of misjudgment or calumny, or of unfair censure, perhaps reproof, or even punishment.
2. The contempt and censure under which he winces seems to be a ban in connection with his religious life, probably a ban against public speech on religious themes. v.23, 'Princes sit and speak against me' — *sit*, i.e. spoken in conclave, or "ex-cathedra", with authority; it is not merely a passing criticism or calumny; v.43 'Take not — he prays — the word of truth *utterly* out of my mouth'. Apparently this had been done partially, i.e. speaking had been restricted.

Further punishment may have been threatened.

3. The contumely to which he had been subjected seems to be associated with his knowledge or possession of the Law, for the two elements — the criticism and his passion for the Word of God — are always linked by "but", "yet", followed by a reiteration of his vow to meditate and the re-affirmation of his delight in the Law of the Lord, His precepts, judgments, instruction, etc. Further punishment threatened could deny him privileges such as access to the Book or even entry to the place of worship, for if his petition is heard, he says he will then "talk" (27), "speak" (46), and he will then "walk at liberty". He speaks of having "declared Thy judgments" (13, 26), and "my lips shall utter Thy praise". (171).

4. The injured tone suggests that he is being persecuted because of or in spite of his knowledge, and he expresses a determination to keep the Law (22 times), that is, by obeying it. His determination is coupled with a plea to God for vindication while again asserting his profound knowledge of and sincere delight in His precepts. This sequence seems to infer that he has been barred from speaking or teaching openly (perhaps in the synagogue) that which to his mind is so clear and delightful. Perhaps he had previously spoken frankly and corrected the misconceptions or tergiversations of the Law in the interpretations traditionally held and taught by scribes, doctors of the Law, etc. cf. "I have declared Thy judgments" (13); "I made haste and delayed not" (60), which suggests that his zeal led to a passionate defence of the truth and he may have openly clashed with them because what he taught condemned their teaching. (97-104, 113-128) or versions of it (141, 151-8, 161). He claims to know more than they all. (97-104).

5. The complaints of persecution coupled with emphatic protestations of his learning and devotion seem to suggest the position of a young man gifted with insight into the beauty and purity of the Law, who, enriched by his constant study of it and by his deep spiritual life, is enabled to understand the more profound meanings of the same, with a maturity beyond his years. His candour and sincere love of the Word and a generous spirit of sharing the "wonderous things out of God's law" (v. 18) that he had

discovered, have been the cause of his clash with men who asserted their authority as teachers of it. (v. 99, 100). This would support the suggestion that it is his youthfulness — and in the eyes of the doctors of the law — his physical immaturity, which has aroused their animostity and caused their censure.

Let us examine this possibility.

Youth and inexperience suggested in the poem.

a) Youth: v.9. The first line of the poem proper (all of the first stanza, vs. 1-8, being introductory): Wherewithal shall a *young man* cleanse his way? — By taking heed to Thy word. — There is always a key word at the opening of the psalm to unlock its meaning.

v. 12. *Teach me* Thy statutes. The request to be taught of God is repeated eight times, in connection with "Thy statutes" (v. 12. 26, 64, 68, 124, 135, 33), good judgment and knowledge (66), Thy judgments (108), and in v. 102, I have not departed from Thy judgments because Thou hast taught me. My lips shall utter Thy praise when Thou hast taught me Thy statutes (171), coming almost at the end of the psalm links up with a similar line near the opening (7): I will praise Thee with uprightness of heart when *I shall have learned* Thy righteous judments. And again, v. 71, It is good for me that I have been afflicted; that *I might learn* Thy statutes. Hence we see that the learning is still in progress in spite of his affirming that (v. 99) I have more understanding than all my teachers, for Thy testimonies are my meditation; and (v. 100), I understand more than the ancients, because I keep Thy precepts. "Thou (v. 98) through Thy commandments hast made me wiser than my enemies!" Here is a mind, conscious of its superiority and at the same time having such a broad scope that it realizes there is more to learn and that his sorrowful experience has given him new insight. We find also that here is a mind greater than the most instructed and learned of his contemporaries or seniors, able to discern greater wealth and penetrate further into the beauty of the Law than they do. Who is this young man, we may ask. Perhaps we should "consider Him who endured such contradiction of sinners against himself", (Heb. 12:3).

This person also prays for "understanding": in v. 27 so that he may "talk of Thy wondrous works"; in v. 34 so he shall keep the law; and (73) learn Thy commandments. He claims his right to ask this — "I am Thy servant: give me understanding, that I may know Thy testimonies," He evidently prays always before studying the Word. "Open Thou mine eyes" (18). He comes to it always because (130) "The entrance of Thy word . . . giveth understanding to the simple"; it certainly does not to the proud or the "gross" (69, 70). "Through Thy precepts I get understanding". It is God who gives him his insight into the Word and the Word that gives him understanding. There is thus a circuit formed between God, the young man who is "Thy servant" and the understanding of the Word. (Father, Son, and Holy Spirit?) God has promised him this: (144). Give me understanding and I shall live; (169) according to Thy word. (If "Thy servant" is the servant of Isaiah's prophecies, it is no wonder that he could say "I understand more than the ancients"! (100). (Before Abraham was I am). Again we find the identity in Heb. 5:8, Though He were a Son, *yet He learned* . . .

When he complains that the proud "have had me in derision *yet* I have not declined from Thy law", we may ask: Was the derision because of his youth? Certainly his knowledge was not to be mocked at. And when he prays (37) "Turn away mine eyes from beholding vanity", was he referring to the vacuous pride of those who held authority? In v. 39 "Turn away the reproach that I fear" — Had they threatened public disgrace? v. 42 . . . So shall I have wherewith to answer him that reproacheth me. — Had they brought false accusations against him and called a tribunal to judge him? v. 43, Take not Thy truth utterly out of my mouth. — Had they attempted to silence him? v. 46, I will speak before kings and not be ashamed. — Had they quoted Proverbs 22:17 to him, "Bow down thine ear and hear the words of the wise", or "Cease from thine own wisdom" (23:4)? His reply could have been, laden with meaning — "The fear of the Lord is the beginning of wisdom, and the knowledge of the Holy is understanding". (Prov. 9:10). v. 53, Horror (anger) because of the wicked that forsake Thy law. — Had he denounced them openly? He states that "I made haste and delayed not" (60), and acknowledges that "It is good for me that I have been afflicted (71). Is this He of Whom it was said, "Thou hast loved righteousness and hated iniquity." (Heb. 1:9; Psa. 45:7) and who *learned by the things that He suffered?*

Another hint of the speaker's youth is that he realizes he still has much to learn. "Teach me", he prays several times, and realizes the need for discipline — It is good for me that I have been afflicted (71). His eager nature makes him seem impatient: How many are the days of Thy servant? When wilt Thou execute judgment? (84). Youthful eagerness, a passionate nature, or messianic urgency — it could be any or all three of theses. His spirit chafes at delay, for he is burgeoning with life like the tree planted by the rivers of water. (Psalm. 1).

He speaks of his present life as "the house of my pilgrimage" (54), showing that he knows life's transcience leads to an abiding home. The same feeling is in v. 19 — "I am a stranger in the earth". He feels an exile from home. May not this sense of urgency have been how the Man sent down from Heaven felt on seeing the need around Him and yet having to wait for the "set time" to begin His task? This thought gives a most touching revelation of His truly human state while it in no way detracts from His divinity and perfection. His human nature and His divine nature were very finely balanced. It gives an insight into the depth and wealth of Jesus' character to realize that He, too, had to impose discipline upon Himself. His strong personality, literally Godlike, had to subdue itself to the limitations imposed upon Him by the circumstances in which God the Father had been pleased to place Him.

b) There is also a sense of *inexperience.* He asks for understanding ten times (insight, prudence). He asks for help and guidance: Deliver me (134, 153, 170); Let my cry — my supplication — come near to Thee. (169-170). Order my steps (133). Let Thine hand help me. (173). Thy testimonies are my counsellors. (24).

He appears not to have had as yet the deep personal experiences of David's psalms — Make me to understand . . . Open mine eyes . . . — though he has evidently had previous experience — Before I was afflicted . . . I cried . . . I entreated Thy favour with my whole heart . . ., — and he has been acquainted with sorrow, humiliation and moral suffering — My soul cleaveth to the dust . . . melteth for heaviness . . . They had almost consumed me . . . Unless Thy law had been my delight I should have perished in affliction . . . Rivers from my eyes . . . Trouble and anguish . . . etc.

He practises the prayer and contemplation during the night watches that characterized Christ when on earth. His feeling is intense — My soul breaketh for the longing that it hath. The exile would find specially precious the recognizable voice of God in His statutes, commandments and precepts, and would cling to them with passionate devotion and longing.

The time span is in the present. The only references to past or future are linked with his resolve to be loyal to God's word: "I will keep", etc., but on occasion he claims the fulfilment of a promise, or expresses his hope in the word pledged. When was that promise given? Not in the experience conveyed in the psalm. Did he find it in the Law, statutes, etc.? If so, why did he claim them as his personally? Is it because HE IS MESSIAH, claiming the pledges given to Him when still with the Father, as we find in other psalms? The picture as a whole is that of a devout soul, a heart determined to understand fully and carry out absolutely all God's commandments, but conscious of the frailness of his humanity. My flesh trembleth for fear of Thee and I am afraid of Thy judgments (I stand in awe of Thy decrees).

He pleads the immutability of God's Word for the fulfilment of certain promises in which he is trusting. — "Remember the word unto Thy servant upon which Thou hast caused me to hope". It appears that the promise he claims is that he should be given life, or be revived, i.e., vouchsafed resurrection, for he implores several times: Quicken me, according to Thy word. This is a plea found especially in the Messianic psalms. Finally, we have seen that in addressing God he refers to himself as "Thy Servant".

Let us now frankly think of him as THE SERVANT, and

a possible prophetic meaning of the psalm in a Messianic context. Let us look again at the facts in this light:

1. Something he has said or done has elicited reproach and contempt from men in authority, "Princes", v. 23; "the proud", v. 51. In men's eyes his affirming his knowledge of the truth looks like presumption, and the fact that he received not merely censure ("reproach") but scorn ("contempt") and derision, would suggest that he was too young in their opinion to set himself up as a teacher, especially if his teachings clashed with their own in the special field which they held to be their domain. cf. v. 51: "derision". They could not have derided the knowledge he evinces in this psalm. The mockery must have been for some other reason. It could have been his youth. Jesus was persecuted by the scribes and Pharisees for daring to disagree with them. (Matt. 13:54). Could their anger not have been the continuation of a long-standing quarrel? They contemptuously call Him "the carpenter's son", pointing out, perhaps, that He was in their eyes an "upstart" trying to enter their ranks.

2. The reproach, or censure, apparently in the form of a punitive or disciplinary action on the part of the "teachers" is grievous to him, for he prays God to turn it away. (v. 39). Worse may have been threatened if he does not submit, for he prays that the reproach he fears (dreads) may be turned away. Jesus had no fear after He had begun His public ministry because He was then a recognized adult, thirty years of age and the sternness of His denunciations suggests a long-contained indignation.

3. The vexed question is evidently one of doctrine, for (42) he prays to be instructed "so I shall have wherewith to answer him that reproacheth me". If it were only mockery or contempt he would neither need nor wish to answer them. When they came to test Jesus (Matt. 6), He quietly ridiculed them. They "asked for a sign from heaven" and He talked to them about what they knew of the clouds! There may have been a ban against the Youth's speaking before His "superiors", i.e. the leaders of the synagogue, doctors of the law. His spirit rises above the hurtful criticism as He prays God to free Him. Far from being prevented from expounding in the presence of the chief priests, I will,

He says, (46) "speak of Thy testimonies also before kings". This means not only a determination to carry out his practice of testifying to the truth, and not only is it a prophecy that Jesus would speak before kings (He did before Herod). It also means that He feels that testifying to God's goodness is His purpose in life, and He will carry out His mission not only then and there but also before men higher in authority than those who have maligned Him. cf "I will not be ashamed" (put to shame). Not that He entertains the possibility of being in error, but that they will not be able to silence Him then or restrict him as they do now.

4. He possesses such integrity of soul and evinces such a full dedication to the Word of God, such single-mindedness in his determination to fulfil and obey every law and precept, that when he has seen others — especially men in authority — flouting it or distorting its meaning, this has horrified and angered him. It may be that in this young man's pure earnestness and eagerness to convince men of the truth, he has refuted erroneous doctrine in the place of worship itself, and has proved by his skilful handling of the Scriptures that the doctors were wrong. ("He taught as one having authority, not as the scribes".) This would madden them into seeking ways and means to prevent his speaking in public. Further, he may have shown the "horror" (53) he felt at the forsaking of the true meaning of the Law, and zealously have denounced the teachings of rabbis. Hear Jesus do so in Matt. 23 and Luke 11.

5. Their retort has been the harsher exercise of their rabbinical powers. They have applied a restraint that deprives him of something he values most highly. (61): "The bands of the wicked have robbed me" — of freedom of speech? Of his privileges? Of his copy of the Law, perhaps? "BUT I have not forgotten Thy law". In other words, I know it by heart (9), I hold it in my memory, hence they cannot take it quite away. That Jesus had a well-stored memory is evident in all His replies.

6. It has been a false accusation (69): The proud have forged a lie against me. Their deceit is falsehood (118). Their policy is to trip him up. Are these enemies the same as those who tried to ensnare Jesus when they came to Him

with their questions? With the simplicity that comes of absolute consecration the speaker sees them as ignorant and "gross" in their mind's intent (70) and he requests that God shall eventually put them to shame, "for they dealt perversely with me without a cause" (78, 161), and "persecute me wrongfully". These statements are closely linked by an affirmation of his devotion introduced by words like "yet", "but", "therefore", with the significance of "however", "in spite of"; and he prays that all those that fear God shall turn to him, that is, decide in his favour, take his side in the coming confrontation. That there would be one is virtually declared, for in the next line he petitions God to "Let my heart be sound in Thy statutes that I be not ashamed". This would suggest that a solemn conclave or tribunal was to be held by those in authority — "Princes" — before whom he would be examined in his knowledge of the Scriptures and challenged in his interpretation of them (his "understanding" of the divine precepts, statutes, testimonies and commandments). Such a conclave may have been held for we can be sure without taking this psalm to contain prophetic connotations — that Jesus did not remain silent about the truth of God's Law until He was thirty years of age. There were in Jesus' time notably narrow Rabbinical schools at Tiberias by the Lake of Galilee, not too far from Nazareth and quite near Capernaum, all places frequented by Him regularly. In David's time of course no such gathering would be held; in Jeremiah's the "princes" were of both the priestly and royal lines. The inference of a tribunal sitting would be applicable in the context to the earlier period, in the Saviour's human life rather than during His public ministry. He may be heard praying for divine instruction and assurance for His replies, and that His memory shall lay hold on the Scripture most apt for their questions, "that I be not put to shame". "Be surety for Thy servant", (122), and again "give me understanding of Thy Word" (169). The urgency is pressing, for it is a "cry", not merely a petition. His request for understanding seems unnecessary in view of his avowed knowledge of "all Thy law" and precepts, unless it is a prayer before an examination in them.

How vividly is suggested here the kind of drama that may

have taken place in Jesus' youth, preceding by many years that adult and authoritative condemnation of the scribes and Pharisees when He attained full manhood and was able to take up the challenge openly! It would explain why there is absolutely no record of anything He said or did between the age of 12 and that of "about thirty". He had assumed His religious adulthood in all seriousness at the age of twelve and He was admitted as such then. With a passionate sense of His mission and a total dedication to "My Father's business", He was burning to start His life's work. But in order to fulfil the law even in this, He was required to await the legal adulthood of the Levite (that is, 30) before He could serve God publicly, in the Temple as it were. (Num. 6 fixes 30 years of age for Aaron's sons and descendants; Num. 8:24 fixes "twenty-five years old and upward" for the Levites in general to enter the service of the tabernacle or temple). That the situation in this psalm belongs to Jesus' youth may be inferred from verses 99 and 100 — "I have more understanding than all my teachers" ... "than the ancients", and the reference to the "young man" at the opening.

Have we in this Psalm the missing page of the history of Jesus' youth? How long has He to wait, He asks, before God vindicates Him? How many are the days of Thy servant? (see Psalm 39). He is eager to begin; time is short. "When wilt Thou execute judgment on them that persecute me?" (84). They have "laid a snare" and "digged pits" for him, probably by the loaded questions they put to Him, as was done later to Jesus on the question of paying tribute to Caesar or on the woman who had seven husbands. In each case it was Jesus' ready knowledge of the Scriptures that produced the unexpected reply that routed them. They would have swept Him from the earth and made an end of Him (87) even as a young man if they could, but (in this and many other psalms) He prays God's loving kindness for the protection of His life, that He might fulfil all of God's Law. "So shall I keep the testimony of Thy mouth".

Again and again the Man of this Psalm refers to the vindictive false accusers. The wicked have waited to destroy me (95); and He prays for deliverance from their machinations: Deliver me from the oppression of man (134).

He seems to turn on them in His heart (as in Psalm 6:8,9) and cries (115) "Depart from me, ye evil doers", leave me alone, "for I WILL keep the commandments of my God". Such an emphatic linking of two apparently unrelated statements suggests the source of the clash, His challengers and critics had wanted to impose on Him other commandments, or their own interpretation of the Law, the traditional teachings of the fathers, and He has rejected it.

After stating (136) that "Rivers of water run down mine eyes because they keep not Thy law", He complains that "My zeal hath consumed me". This Young Man had been deeply pained at seeing the Law He loved distorted by the teachers and openly flouted. Perhaps they had been sharp when He showed His superior knowledge, and He had insisted that His interpretaion of the Law was the correct one. This had brought the trouble upon Him. My zeal hath consumed me *because* mine enemies have forgotten Thy words (139). They had lost sight of the true meaning of the Law. Additions had accrued that were not part of the original truth. "Thy word" (140), He says, "is very pure, therefore Thy servant loveth it". One version has translated "My zeal hath consumed me" as "my indignation" . . . a sentiment which runs through the whole poem. In the same stanza another personal admission throws light on the position: "I am small and despised yet I do not forget Thy precepts (141). If we see this as meaning "young" as well as "of no repute", the idea again seems to be that it was His youthfulness that they resented as well as His self-assurance in His knowledge. In other words it was His supposed presumption that infuriated them and caused their enmity. There seems to be another hint of the reason for the clash in the syntax "yet do not I forget", instead of the usual negative form. Perhaps He means that His accusers have been the ones to "forget Thy precepts", which would substantiate the meaning inferred in the "because" above. He is conscious of His moral ascendency over them on the grounds of His total adherence to the Law as God gave it to Moses. Here "Let us consider the Apostle and High Priest of our profession, Christ Jesus, who was faithful to Him that appointed Him". The parallels lie mainly in a) the unmerited antagonism and persecution; b) the declaration of His obedience to God, c) a sense of the need to affirm that He is "Thy servant'.

It appears in the poem that the mishandling of the holy precepts by those who persecute this Youth wounds Him very deeply. It is not only that men attack His rendering of the Law, but that His detractors' erroneous doctrine mutilates the divine truth or distorts its true meaning, and this causes Him pain. He has mentioned the "rivers of water" that flow from His eyes (136) at men's departure from God's Law. Now (158) "I beheld the transgressors and was grieved, because they kept not Thy word". His "eyes prevent the night watches". The thought of their erroneous representation of God to the people makes Him writhe all night. His watching is not stated in a context of enjoyment in meditation as before, for instance (55) "I have remembered Thy name, O Lord, in the night"; or (62) "At midnight I will rise to give thanks unto Thee . . ." Now (145-152) it is associated with His distress — "I cried with my whole heart . . . I cried unto Thee, Save me . . . I prevented the dawning of the morning and cried, I hope (for the fulfilment of) Thy word. Hear me", he implores, "according to Thy loving kindness. O Lord, quicken me . . . They draw nigh that follow after mischief' — but it is not only his enemies who draw nigh (151): "Thou art near, O Lord", he adds.

Once more, in the final stanza (169-176), He prays to be heard and asks to be given understanding. He supplicates God for deliverance. From what? one wonders. The lines that follow may tell: "My lips shall utter praise, my tongue shall speak of Thy word." If we are to understand any logical sequence here it must be a prayer for deliverance from penalizing restrictions on speech, perhaps a ban against public participation in worship. When Jesus was called to His public ministry and entered the synagogue for the first time after the Temptation, they handed Him the Book and "He found the place where it was written, The Spirit of the Lord is upon me . . ." — and He read His call to service, after which "He closed the book, and gave it again to the minister, and sat down and began to teach". The details recorded show that He knew how to "find the place" in that scroll, and the correct procedure. (Luke 4:14-

21). Mark adds (Peter was probably present) that "He taught as one having authority" (1:22). That would be equally true on the occasion we are supposing to have caused all this expostulation, distress, supplication and the affirmation of His knowledge of the Law in Psalm 119. Matthew records (15:1-9) how He answered the criticism of the scribes and Pharisees with the challenging question — "Why do ye also transgress the commandment of God by your tradition? For God commanded, saying . . . But ye say . . . thus ye have made the commandment of God of none effect by your tradition". This is exactly what is hinted at in the Psalm. Jesus then called them hypocrites and quoted Isaiah to the effect that they were "teaching for doctrine the commandments of men". The disciples warn Him, "Knowest Thou not that the Pharisees were offended at this saying?" Yes, He certainly did know! He answers, from His experience: "Let them alone: they be blind leaders of the blind". He had already tried to open their eyes to the light and they had loved darkness rather than light, because their deeds were evil. (John 3:19).

But before we go any further v. 67 requires careful attention: "Before I was afflicted I went astray, but now I have kept Thy word". As an admission of error or disobedience or even ignorance this verse is not applicable to the Lord Jesus. He never knew sin until on the Cross those of the world were laid upon Him. But by imaginatively associating the whole psalm with a personal experience of our Lord, there is a possible explanation which does not entail the thought of sin. Since Jesus was Holiness in Person sin was impossible, but temptation was not. Might the driving Power in His divine nature and the innate authority to Him instinctive, require to be disciplined and controlled? Divine wrath, indignation, even zeal in the Child had to come under restraint. When, for instance, at the age of 12 He apparently believed that the time had come to step out from under His guardians' care and be about His heavenly Father's business, this decision having arisen in Himself in Godlike independence, might this in retrospect have seemed to His holy mind as something that had been brought under subjection? This incident may have illustrated the native impulse of princely resolution in His spirit to which He never again gave rein. He had to learn that He could not decide for Himself. He was the Word that was with God and was God; but His divine Nature had to learn to accept the limitations of His human frame and His position as Servant. This was an entirely new experience. His character was flawless but "he *learned obedience*". The exuberant nature of the Tree planted by rivers of water had to be subject to the will of the Father at every stage.

It is interesting to speculate what may have been the "affliction" of which the poet speaks, as applied to the human Christ: "It is good for me that I have been afflicted, that I might learn Thy statutes". (71) perhaps it was a very great disappointment for the 12-year-old Jesus who had just attained religious adulthood, to leave what He believed to be His Father's business and go back to the northern provincial village where there were no learned men to talk to, and to be subject to Joseph again, and where, as helper in the earning of the family's living, He was not free to go out over the land preaching and teaching as He hoped to do. But the occasion referred to is in the recent past: ". . . that I have been afflicted". The affliction could also have been the ordeal which is suggested in this Psalm.

In His early twenties — He, having not as yet received the command to go forth to His public ministry — must have had experiences in His relations with the rabbis and teachers of the Law which taught Him to suppress in certain circumstances His God-like authority because the time for it had not yet come. Jesus was God, and — one says it reverently — He had to learn to be Man. That it cost Him many a tear we may deduce from Psalm 119.

This Psalm ends on a rather plaintive note: "I have gone astray like a lost sheep; seek Thy servant: for I do not forget Thy commandments". Now the author of a psalm that reiterates his familiarity with and passionate devotion to the Law, judgments and commandments of the Lord, could not have strayed from the path he knew and loved so well. The meaning in modern translations is clearer: I feel alone like a sheep lost in the wilderness . . .

The whole context of the Psalm quite excludes the interpretation of "gone astray" as a straying from the right path. The author's earlier statements of feeling a stranger

(19) and an alien (54) in the world, which comes to a head here, asserts his sense of isolation. If this verse is to be seen *in its context* and the feeling of separation as also part of the Son's experience, then we realize that it is His solitariness precisely as a sinless Being, not certainly any sense of wrong-doing, that is emphasized here. "... for I *do not forget* Thy commandments".

As a youth Jesus must have realized how set apart He was; in the world but not of it. The present situation is alien to Him, so different from His accustomed environment in Heaven. The ostracism inferred throughout the poem (both for the author and for the Young Man prophetically described) imposed by the priests and elders who were angered at his (and Jesus') daring to refute their doctrine, as He probably did even in His youth, would make His solitariness the more felt. He must often have felt a sorrow as of exile. The expression of "going astray" or "wandering" has connotations in our mind that do not apply to His, His purity and sinlessness being indisputable. It is here a *figure of speech* denoting a deep sense of isolation and dereliction. And here is the deepest and most moving inference. For the letter which heads this last stanza, TAU, is the old form of the cross and means mark, brand. Surely the explanation lies here. The psalmist, moved by the Holy Spirit, and in despite of all his protestations of uprightness throughout the poem, was compelled to carry the account of an Upright Life to an unforeseen conclusion which in the designs of God included the Cry from the Cross, "Why hast thou forsaken ME?" The prophetic spirit descending on the psalmist caused him to make a like exclamation, his rendering of it being, "I feel lost, alone as a lost sheep: Seek Thy servant, for I do not forget Thy commandments". The prayer was answered. Jesus was raised from the dead and returned to glory but the "TAU" imprinted by the Cross will forever remain on His Body.

The last verse, therefore, is not an anticlimax, nor does it contradict all the previous statements of adherence to the divine ordinances. The situation of which he complains throughout the psalm is here shown in its pathos and the image of the solitary Lamb catches up in synthesis the tone of the whole, linking the end with the beginning, for the occasion is still present. When, on the annual ceremony of the nation's sin-offering the scapegoat was sent away into the wilderness, unto a land not inhabited, did there cross His soul a premonitory shadow of the future act when He would bear upon Himself the sins of the people?

The problem he faces has not yet been solved, the experience is not over; there is no emergence from the trial which threatened nor any hint as to the historical outcome. If he rises above it, it is by faith, for "I have hoped in Thy judgments" (43), and He claims "the word unto Thy servant upon which Thou hast caused me to hope" (49). "This is my comfort in my affliction: for Thy word that quickened me" (50). He believes in a favourable outcome for He states with assurance that "They that fear Thee will be glad when they see me because I have hoped in Thy word" (74). The highest emotional peak in the poem is the cry: "O how I love Thy law! It is my meditation all the day" (103) "Thou art my portion, O Lord" (57) acquires a deeper significance when seen in this context. It infers: I have no one and nothing else, yet what want I more.

One would like to know if Jesus had a copy of the Law of His own. There were not many complete copies of the Scriptures in existence, yet He is familiar not only with the Books of Moses but quotes from most of the Prophets. Even the synagogue would probably only have one or two scrolls beside the "Law". Joseph and Mary must have instructed Him, for when He was twelve He already showed so thorough a knowledge of the Scriptures that he was able to debate with the doctors in the Temple. His knowledge would not be by miraculous prescience. He had read and had had to memorize them; He had thought about them. Perhaps as Head of the House of Judah His family possessed a complete copy, one enjoined to the king to make personally. (Duet. 17:18). Did He learn to write by making a copy of the Law as Moses commanded? We do not know. But it seems very probable that some of His meditations therein and the opposition He encountered are in Psalm 119, prophetically recorded. He kept the precepts, to the glory of God the Father.

Psalm 119 answers the question the elders put to each other in the synagogue: "Whence hath this man this wisdom?" (Matt. 13:54). Jesus' own answer was, "My doctrine is not mine, but His that sent me". (John 7:15, 16). His cry "Teach me" had been heard and the Father spake by His Son, but He, Jesus, acquired knowledge also by His profound study of the Scriptures, His unreserved devotion to their truth, and a submission to their discipline.

One recalls having read that the Hebrew alphabet tells pictorially the story of the Exodus. May it not be that the choice of the alphabetic acrostic in this Psalm also hints at the story of the pilgrimage of the Righteous Man Who is the Hero of all the Psalms?

In many points this Psalm is prophetic of Christ's adult experiences, especially that He was held in contempt by those who were "teachers" but who were themselves grossly ignorant of the truth while the Victim of their censure exceeded them in the knowledge of God's Law. In fact an incident from the Gospel records could be cited to substantiate and illustrate every one of the complaints in this Psalm. But though events recorded in the Gospels prove the prophetic value of this Psalm, they cover only the period of Jesus' maturity and authority. What in the Psalm is very discernible is that a situation, which could be an unusually precocious wisdom, was what caused the rupture with the "teachers" as well as possible disagreement over doctrine in His youth. The latter factor seems to be inferred in Psalm 119, but the former is uppermost. Hence, though the Psalm could be held as prophetic of Jesus' public experience in adulthood, it might well be so of the unrecorded years of His life and thus offer a picture which fills the gap in the narrative of Jesus' life on earth.